STAND UP AND BE A LADY

ROBIN SAVAGE

Published 2014 by HumorOutcasts Press
Printed in the United States of America

ISBN 0-692-26688-7
EAN-13 978-069226688-5

Cover Design by Joe Hetro

ACKNOWLEDGMENTS

I want to thank and acknowledge the following people for helping me write this book:

Donna Cavanagh and HumorOutcast Press – I am grateful that you took a chance on me by publishing Stand Up and Be a Lady.

Julie Ross – I appreciate your wonderful editing skills and rifling through my rants to help me find my voice.

Joe Hetro – You are a great artist that created and designed an awesome book cover.

My family, both real and extended Savannah family- You provided me with years of love, laughter and crazy stories.

My extended comedy family- Thank you for teaching me how to be funny on stage and for making so many memorable nights. Also to Mary Tischbein thanks for the wonderful Foreword. It has been a pleasure sharing the comedy stage with you.

Finally to my children – You are responsible for the light in my life, the sparkle in my eye and the sticky on my furniture.

Foreword

"Say your name for me again…?"

I met Robin Savage at a second rate comedy club's open mic night on a Thursday in the fall of 2008. I was brand new to performing; she was a year and change ahead of me. Robin was emceeing and did not want to mispronounce my last name, it was important to her to show me the proper respect as a performer. The thing is, I really didn't deserve any respect yet. I was a newbie—a grunt, but Robin knew we all had something in common. We all thought, for some crazy reason, that we could do it, be real comedians, just like our heroes: Carol Burnett, Tracey Ullman, and Ellen DeGeneres. Even though it was early on in the game, we were in it for the long haul.

Robin recognized that drive to succeed in each of us that night. She knew we all deserved a chance, and a little respect, and she gave it to us, even if it meant just pronouncing our names correctly in our intro. I'm sure other professional comedians had shown Robin respect early on, but that is not something she learned from them. It was instilled in her at an early age, and she was raised right. Being a good old girl from the Midwest is something Robin claims with pride. That's one of the traits that makes Robin unique in standup, her desire to not discount anyone, no matter who they are or who they appear to be—no matter what the gossip is and no matter where they are from. Everybody gets a shot.

Robin took her job as host of the open mic show seriously. She kept reviewing the lineup sheet and checked in with each of us to let us know who we were following and when our turn was coming up. Her smile, firm handshake and attention to detail struck me as rare in comedy. I had only met a few comics so far, and she was the kindest, most professional—and get this—a lady! It's a man's world! But that's a whole different book.

A few months later, some other newbies and I started a little showcase at a coffee shop in Bradenton, FL, where I was living at the time. I called Robin and asked her to join us, to give our little venture some legitimacy. She drove an hour, all the way from Tampa, which now seems like nothing but back then I thought, "Wow! She is willing to travel all that way. Good for her!"

Another opportunity presented itself at a local cabaret, and I contacted Robin again. From there we started an all-female comedy troupe that helped us all stretch our material, learn how to properly market shows and as a result, friendships were cemented. We had a three year run. Good times.

Through all the ups and downs of pursuing excellence in an art form (yes, standup comedy is art), one thing remained: the desire to make people laugh. Robin's writing ability always foretold of more than just joke-writing. Not that her comedy writing isn't stellar, she always makes me laugh when she is onstage. Her easy going persona and physicality are a natural fit in standup comedy. Robin has that 'IT' factor they talk about. She would not admit it, but it's not something that can be denied.

I am proud to say that Robin rewrote one of my weaker jokes and turned it into a strong crowd pleasing bit. We were discussing it on the way to a gig. She thought about it for a second and had the solution. I still use in every performance. Come to a show, and I'll tell you which one it is.

Even though I don't get to work with Robin Savage as much as I did in the beginning of my little comedy career, I have fond memories of all those shows. Whether we were at a bar, club or corporate gig, whether we were performing as a troupe, as alternating feature and headliner or even co-headliners, I always knew the night was going to bring surprises, fun and definitely laughs because Robin Savage was going to be on the show that night, and she's awesome.

I am truly honored to have been asked to write this introduction to my friend's book. I hope you enjoy reading it as much as I have enjoyed my friendship with its author. May the words make you think, learn and laugh, just as Robin has always done for me.

May this book be another step in the right direction for Robin Savage's dream quest. Buckle up and get ready to guffaw.

Mary Tischbein
Comedian

Table of Contents

MY ADVENTURES IN COMEDY

Chapter One
The Trouble With Tremors

Firsts are always memorable. They may not be great, but you always remember your first kiss, your first time getting drunk, and the first time making the sweet and tender nooky, which, hopefully, were three separate occasions. Stand up comedy is no different. My first time on stage was terrifying. I was afraid of shaking in front of people, I was afraid of not being funny, and I was afraid of looking really stupid. When the time finally came, all three happened on the same occasion.

What I didn't expect was the adrenaline rush. Doing stand up comedy for the first time is a lot like riding a roller coaster. You close your eyes, take a big gulp, and let out a blood-curdling scream the entire time, but when the ride stops, you want to go back again and again.

There is something about making people laugh that is very addicting. It is attention, affection, and power, all in the same response. When you realize that your words can cause a visceral reaction in other people, it is pretty amazing. It makes you feel that your sense of humor is your life's calling. It's like the ending scene of the movie "Boogie Nights" (spoiler alert for anyone who hasn't seen the 1997 flick). Dirk Diggler, the porn star played by actor Marky Mark, exposes his enormous penis, and you realize that to him, his huge wiener is the greatest gift he has to offer the world. In the story, Dirk is being used in the worst of ways, by the worst of people, but he sees his giant endowment as something that makes him unique and worthy of love. This scene breaks my heart on a million different levels, but every person who thinks of themselves as funny feels about their humor the way Dirk does about his giant schlong. It is our secret weapon against the world. It is our blessing that makes us stand out from everyone else. It is the essence of what makes us special.

When I was a kid, I didn't have a lot going for me. My brother Olin—who's four years older than me—was the smart one. I was a tomboy and had no interest in being a "girly-girl." After I turned eight, my wavy blond hair turned brown, course, and unruly curly and my complexion began to resemble a large Meat Lover's Pizza. Needless to say, Mother Nature pretty much concurred that beauty wasn't going to be my path in life. I was always funny, though. I remember being in second grade and doing an impression of Jimmy Carter during recess. In hindsight, I was actually doing an impression of Dan Akroyd's Jimmy Carter, but I remember it being a hit. I was high-strung and constantly talking. The television show "Mork and Mindy" was popular at the time. My classmates starting calling me "Mork." I am not sure if it was meant to be an insult or not, but I took it as the highest of compliments. I even had my Mom buy me rainbow suspenders. In my extremely awkward adolescent years to come, I would wonder why I was never asked out much. This should have been a huge clue.

In addition to all my quirky personality issues, I also have a neurological condition called Essential Tremor. It makes me shake like a leaf on a good day. When my adrenaline gets pumping, I tremble uncontrollably. I can't remember not shaking, even as a little kid. The doctors told my parents it was hypoglycemia, so for a long time I couldn't eat any sugar. People—adults and children alike—would always comment on my quivering hands. I remember getting my feelings hurt a few times when kids at school teased me about it. I got good at avoiding games like "Operation," the egg toss, and "Jenga", the most heartless of all activities for those with a movement disorder. You may ask how playing a game like "Jenga" could possibly be a stressful activity. That's easy. It requires players to take turns removing one block at a time from a tower constructed of 54 blocks. Each block removed is then balanced on top of the tower, to create a progressively taller, but less stable, structure. No one ever wanted me to be on their Jenga team at a party, because the shaking of the table by my trembling hands would have toppled the tower before I even took my turn.

I kept hoping my tremors were something that I would outgrow, something from which I could move on. That never happened. I remember getting frustrated and thinking I would never get past the shaking. In some ways, I never have. I still have the tremors. They only seem to get worse with age. I have grown to hate them. I hate my tremors in the same way that I hate my allergies. They are both two internal forces within my body trying to dictate what I can and can't do. Sometimes I want to rebel against my own anatomy—rough it up in a back alley, let it know that I am charge, demand it stop being a bully. "Fuck you, body…you don't know me."

I remember the first time I realized that being funny could be rewarded in school, rather than get me sent to sit in the hallway after being "hilarious" in the classroom.

When Olin was in high school, he joined the Forensics and Debate team. He was fantastic. He was the LeBron James of debating. He was a beast at both the pros and the cons, and he could do rebuttals like a champ. He would always win. It was apparent that he was having his Dirk Diggler moment when, ever-formidable in his dark gray JC Penney suit, he destroyed his opponents one by one.

I enjoyed watching Olin, but I thought the actual debating part was boring. I would sometimes watch other people who did Forensics and thought it looked like fun. It was acting with just one person. The Forensics participants recited poetry, prose, and dramatic and humorous monologues. So when I started high school, I joined the Forensics team. I was hoping that this would be the avenue that would validate that I had a real gift. I could prove to the world that I was indeed funny and not just the class clown. My "Boogie Nights dick" was trying to peek out.

I competed in the fables and storytelling division. I found an old Swedish fable about wind and why wind blows from different directions. The winds in the story were personified, and I gave each one its own accent. I made the West wind have a surfer accent, while the South wind had a drawl, the Northern wind was Canadian, and the East coast wind was a wicked awesome Bostonian. I thought it was very clever. Unfortunately, my tremor was still very present. I would always get last place because the judges had seen the shaking and interpreted the tremor as anxiety. On my evaluations, they'd write comments like "Don't be so nervous" and "She was shaking the whole time."

Also in my freshman year of high school, the Drama Club decided instead of doing a long play that they would do "An Evening of One Acts." I tried out for the lead in one of the comedies, called "The Man in the Bowler Hat." My role was Mary, a frumpy housewife with a boring husband who has to confront and apprehend an intruder in their house. I was worried that my shaking would prevent me from getting the role. I decided to just to go balls to the wall and give it all I had. If I didn't get the part, at least I would have tried my best. It has been 30 years, and I still remember the huge laughs at the audition. I asked the drama teacher about my shaking. She said as long as I had my lines memorized and my blocking correct, no one could really notice it from the stage. She was right. I got the part. It was a great run for two weekends in my little high school. One of the teachers said that watching me was like watching a young Carol Burnett. What a compliment!

I remember thinking that maybe I had finally found my destiny. I dropped out of Forensics and took Drama class in my sophomore year. The teacher from the year before had quit. A new teacher had taken her place. The new teacher wasn't very attractive and couldn't say her "R's." She talked like the cartoon character Elmer Fudd. I remember not liking her at all, and I wondered how a person with a noticeable impairment could try to be a performer. The fact that I was a weird-looking teenager with a tremor was lost on me, and the irony that she was kind of like me didn't occur to me until I got older. I didn't stick with Drama. I went on to making hanging out with my friends and being the class clown my main priority in high school.

But as the years went by, I found myself still performing in front of people. There was something about being in front of a crowd that kept drawing me in. In my late twenties, I had climbed my way up the corporate ladder by a rung or two. I had a thankless, shitty call center job and managed to get promoted to a trainer position. I learned how to use politically correct language to teach loads of other people how to work a thankless, shitty call center job, but I was being paid to speak in front of people. It wasn't theater, it wasn't stand up, but I could still make people laugh.

Initially being a trainer was fun, but it was very stressful. My first class began to notice my shaking. Rather than asking me about it, a bunch of students went in as a group to Human Resources. They wanted to complain that I was trembling. The class had observed it as a sign of weakness. Human Resources went to my boss, who ripped them a new one. She wanted to know why HR hadn't asked the students if they had approached me about the tremors. Had HR asked me about the tremors? From then on, I was instructed to inform each new class that I had Essential Tremor.

It was humiliating. I didn't know how to bring it up. "Hey, class full of newly hired employees, I have something wrong with my brain that makes me shake as a reaction to my own adrenaline. Now who wants to hear about their benefits package?" I kept wondering whether, if I were in a wheelchair or had missing limbs, I would be asked to address that before every class of new hires.

I was a trainer for only five years. My life continued to evolve, and I eventually had two children with my husband. I stayed home with the babies initially. My son and daughter are only 19 months apart. I love them with all of my heart and soul, but being at home and devoting myself only to caring for them was slowly driving me crazy. One Sunday afternoon, I was looking through the newspaper and saw a schedule for a local performing arts center. I'd been thinking about a toddler music or dance class for my then-two-year-old son, but suddenly I noticed information about an adult stand up comedy class. Something in my head told me that if I didn't try it right then, I never would. It was the same little voice I'd been ignoring for years. I could usually shut it up by justifying and procrastinating, but now it was now calling my bluff…. "Come on, you Pussy! Are you ever gonna put your money where your mouth is? You think you are so funny and so special, but you've never tried stand up comedy, not even once…it's now or never. Are you gonna be someone or just someone's Mom for the rest of your life?" My voice in my head can be a dick sometimes.

I took the class. At first, I didn't even tell my husband it was a stand up class. He thought it was just another class that I was taking in my endless pursuit to get my Bachelors degree—which I still haven't earned. I didn't tell him because I wanted an "escape" clause or one of those "chicken" exits that they have on the roller coaster lines at amusement parks. I wasn't a hundred percent sure that I had the chutzpah to actually go through with it. I performed in class for the first time and confessed to my husband that it was stand up class I was attending on Monday nights. After performing in class, I went to one open mic, then another and another and another. Stand up went from being an escape/hobby to being a calling. I soon began emceeing and then featuring. I even occasionally headline. My tremors have been a constant battle all the while. I noticeably shook when I was a novice. I have tried every approach to deal with it. I've held the mic with one hand, held it with two hands. I've not held it all and kept it in the stand. I've written and performed material about shaking, and other times I've gone on stage and never uttered a word about it. I've consulted other comics. In the end, I've just gotten so comfortable with being on stage now that the tremors lessen. I still deal with them in my daily life, but when I have a mic in my hand and hear the laughter, nothing else seems to matter. It is like the happiness of soul trumps the limitations of my body.

The big picture of my life is pretty amazing. I have a great family, a few people I can call true friends, and a gift for making others laugh. Just as in "Boogie Nights," my show will go on. I'll strut my stuff and display my prowess for all the world to see.

Chapter Two
Standing in Front of Naked People

Four times in my life, I have performed comedy in front of a crowd of naked people. I was dressed, but the audience wasn't. You would think it would be the opposite of stripping, but it's not. I am still the vulnerable one. The crowd, clothed or unclothed, has the power to crush or inflate my ego. With stripping, it is about raw sexuality. With comedy, it is about invoking laughter with your words, but in this case, it happens while looking at exposed genitals.

The first time I was asked to perform comedy to an "au natural" crowd was at a clothing-optional resort. A local comedy booker was contracting his "club" out to one of the many nudist communities in the area. Rather than trouble these folks with the unpleasant task of putting on pants and coming to a comedy show, the booker was going to bring the comedy show to them and have a once-a-week "Comedy Night" in the bar located in front of the lobby.

The booker first approached me about being the house emcee, which meant I would have hosted the show every week. The idea was tempting: Guaranteed stage time every Friday night, and the pressure to write new stuff every week rather than get lazy and just depend on my reliable material from my set. The fact that everyone would have been unclad really didn't faze me that much. I could get my comedy fix. It is the same way a smoker accidentally breaks his last cigarette, but figures out a way to rig it so it can be smoked anyway. Yeah, maybe a naked audience wasn't ideal, but it was still an audience.

The booker chose me because I am a clean comic and despite the fact that the clientele walked around in their birthday suits, they were supposedly not fans of vulgarity. I found all of this to be a hoot. I came home and told my husband about it. He wanted to come along, not so much to see me perform, but to ogle strange, naked women. After decades of being in a relationship with me, I could not be any more sympathetic to his cause. I told him that I just had to go the first night and do a five-minute guest set, and that the booker was going to emcee the initial show, but after this night, I would be the house emcee. I told my husband that he could go on any other night after that. What could go wrong? Could I do something so offensive, it would ruin my opportunity to be a regular there? Yeah, right. (Eye roll).

My husband, in his glee to see any bare lady's breasts other than mine, told our neighbor about the impending gig. My neighbor then told me that he had read that this particular resort had recently been busted for having Swinger parties. I was ecstatic! I had a whole bit about Swingers. It was really the dirtiest of my jokes, but wasn't considered vulgar, as it was all innuendo. How could a room full of Swingers not like jokes about Swingers?

When I first arrived there, the resort itself looked pretty fancy. Had there not been naked people walking around, I would have thought it was a Disney hotel. The landscaping was perfectly manicured, and the buildings onsite were big and well-maintained. The actual room that the comedy was held in was beautiful. It was really two rooms. One was part was a large, rectangular-shaped bar that was adjacent to a larger open room with a stage on one side. The stage was enormous. You had to walk up six or seven steps to get on it, and it attached to it was a full-blown DJ booth, complete with a live DJ who acted as the audio guy throughout the show. Directly in front of the stage was the dance floor, with tables set up around it. That was my only real complaint about the setup. The audience wouldn't be directly in front of me; they would be looking at me across an empty dance floor. Other than that, it was a really nice venue.

As far as the people went, none of nudists were attractive. When I thought about seeing a group of naked people, I pictured a bunch of hotties. In my mind's eye, the room was going to be filled with Matthew McConaugheys and Jennifer Anistons, all beautiful and fit. That isn't what happened. It was like going into Wal-mart and seeing those people in the buff. No one was young or "Hollywood fit." They were just every day, run-of-the-mill people. I became of huge fan of clothes after that experience.

To be fair, not everyone was naked. Some people just walked around half-naked, some were partially clad, and others were dressed like strippers or prostitutes, which really isn't that shocking when other people were exposing it all. I thought it was funny to see the men wearing just shirts and no pants. My whole life, I had seen men wear only shorts and no tops. The opposite seemed kind of feminine to me, in a weird way.

The resort also appeared to have a rule that if you sat down anywhere while you were naked, you had to put a towel underneath yourself. The "bottoms-free" people had towels slung over their shoulders wherever they went. I guess that rule was for hygiene. It would have left a horrible snail trail had people just sat with their bare undercarriages anywhere and everywhere. Still, I wondered if there was a special health inspector dedicated to nude establishments. I imagined a restaurant filled with a cooking staff, all with nothing on but hair nets, and a stern man in a three-piece suit walking around with a clipboard. He is the Naked Restaurant Health Inspector. They are all nervous.

"What is this?" demands the inspector, pointing to an open container. "Has this cheese been sitting out longer than 30 minutes?"

"No, sir," replies some lowly food prep guy, quickly washing his hands, then putting Saran wrap on the container and returning it to the refrigerator. His balls flap all the while as he scurries around the kitchen.

The inspector's stoic expression slowly turns to a smile. "Great job, you folks really know hygiene," he says. The kitchen explodes in cheers. The staff all jump up and down while their pubic hair remains exposed. The End.

While I was trying to acclimate myself to these surroundings, I spotted the evening's headliner, "Kit Handsome." I had known him for several years. His attitude about the resort was different than mine. He wasn't amused by any of it.

"What a bunch of elitist rich mother fuckers," he said. "I know these types. They act like they are such purists, and none of this is sexual. What bullshit."

"Have you really looked at these people, though?" I replied. "I think it just permanently decreased my sex drive by about 65%."

While we were talking, an older man with a fishnet tank top, no bottoms, and a towel slung over his shoulder struck up a conversation with another partially-clad woman in front of us. Midway through the conversation, the man dropped the keys he had been jiggling in his hands (Where else would he have put them? He didn't have pockets, after all), so he bent over and picked them up. That's right, no bottoms, an old man, and a wide-open butt. Kit and I simultaneously groaned and looked away.

When it came time to do the actual comedy show, I was the second person to take the stage. The booker, as promised, did 10 or so minutes and explained to the crowd that this was going to be a regular weekly show. The crowd seemed appreciative, maybe a little tight, meaning it was a little bit difficult to make them laugh, but they seemed ready for a good time.

When I took the stage, I opened with a line that I had come up with earlier in the week: "So, I hear you guys would give the shirts off your backs for a good comedy show!" The crowd loved it. I got huge laughs. I always feel that I can breathe a little easier when I get that first big laugh right away. In my mind, I thought, "If they loved this, wait until they hear my Swinger material." I began: "So, I hear you guys are ALL swingers here? ..." On and on I went. Instead of uproarious laugher, I got silence--awful, gut wrenching, deafening silence. Granted, I was only supposed to do a five-minute set, but when you die on stage 30 seconds into your act, five minutes seems like an eternity—a long, tortuous eternity.

I did all of my time, but I started sweating and continued to get my zero laughs from the crowd. I had no idea what I had done wrong, but I knew it was something.

When I was finished and gave the mic back to the booker, he did the standard, "Let's hear it one more time for Robin Savage." Even that barely garnered any applause. I had started walking down the steps off the stage, when the headliner grabbed me by the elbow and whisked me away to the back of the club.

"You really fucked up, Robin," Kit warned me.

"You're not kidding!" I replied. "What did I do?"

"Apparently, they don't like being called Swingers," he stated.

"But my neighbor told me that they were Swingers and got busted for it," I defended myself, growing a little scared. "It made the Internet news."

I had sensed before when an audience disliked me, but never to the point that another comic felt the need to physically escort me away from the crowd.

"While you were on stage, some lady came up to me and said 'We aren't Swingers. There was a small group of people that got in trouble, but that doesn't represent who we are,'" Kit explained to me.

"Oh, I guess my neighbor didn't read that part." I said meekly. At this point, I was starting to get genuinely concerned. "What should I do? Should I just leave?"

"No," the headliner said. "Fuck them. You're a comic. This is a comedy show. Sit down next to me at the bar. Drink a beer like you don't give a shit about them or what they think." Kit is from Boston and has that East Coast, cool-guy persona about him, which as a Midwesterner is very hard to duplicate.

"Sure, I can do that," I answered. My tremor was kicking in double-time at this point.

We sat down at the bar, and I ordered a beer. I was watching the middle act, trying to feign aloofness, when there was a tap on my shoulder. It was a hefty woman, who fortunately was clothed.

"Honey, let me give you a little advice" she said. "You need to do your homework. We are not a bunch of Swingers here. You may have heard about a few people, but we don't appreciate being called Swingers."

I kept my hands at my sides so she couldn't see me shaking. "That's cool," I told her. "That bit is a part of my act that I usually do it at the end of my set. I thought I would try it out here. I guess I was wrong. It happens." I acted as if this was a conversation that I normally had. I said it with no more remorse than if I had been discussing fabric softeners—all the while planning my escape in my head.

"Well I thought you were funny," she said, backing down a little, "but some people around here didn't find it that funny. You just REALLY need to do your homework better next time."

"I see your point. Cool. Thanks."

The lady left. I was terrified.

"Are you sure I shouldn't just take off, right now?" I whispered to Kit.

"No. Fuck that," he told me. "Who does that bitch think she is? 'Do your homework.' I hate these rich elitist mother fuckers."

I stayed for the rest of the show. Kit, as usual, killed it. He had them laughing for his entire set, and all was fine by the end of the night. I decided not to leave early, if for nothing else than to prove that I didn't care about the thing that was actually giving me a stomach ache. I never heard back from the booker about being the house emcee again.

I had all but written off the nudist resort when I got a call about a year and a half later, asking me to fill in for a last-minute guest spot. My initial reaction was to not do it. By this time, the recession had almost destroyed my profession. The booker had gone from paying the headliner and feature to only paying headliners and just calling the feature spots "extended guest sets." On that very principle, I didn't want to be a part of it.

But in the back of my mind, there lay a feeling of regret over the whole Swinger joke debacle. I had a secret hope to do that room over again, to get a comedy mulligan. I hate bombing. It eats away at my soul. In my feeble comic's mind, I kept rationalizing: "It wasn't really me that they hated. It was my assumption of who I thought they were that they hated. Had I not insulted the very core of their belief system, they would have found me adorable." So, being the pathetic comedy-addict that I am, agreed to play the club again.

The second time wasn't the Rocky-esque story that I had secretly hoped for. There was no full-circle moment where they loved me. I did about 15 minutes, sans the Swinger material, and did alright. They laughed at all the places that I wanted them to. I have done better, but they didn't hate me, and I wasn't afraid about a possible attack by an angry (naked) mob after my set. All in all, it felt like a small victory for me.

As it always happens in comedy, nothing stays the same. Eventually, the original booker had a falling out with the clothing-optional resort. Comedy Night stopped for awhile and was taken over by someone else. The new booker wasn't just a comic; he was also a nudist who paid comics to do the feature sets. So when I was asked a third time to come back, bad experience or not, I didn't turn down a paid gig.

Although they say that a third time is a charm, this third time was more of an aphrodisiac wrapped in hormones and dipped in the party drug Molly. This particular show was on the Friday night prior to Memorial Day weekend, and the whole place was drunk, naked, and making out with each other in groups. Being that several years had passed, I don't know if the conservative people were no longer predominately a part of the community or if they weren't at this show, but these people were wired! I don't know what an orgy actually smells like, but the pre-orgy seemed to have a lot of vodka fumes.

When I went on stage, I had their attention for awhile, but as I continued, their interest waned. They were more concerned about groping one another in public. "Fuck it," I thought to myself. "I am going to go for the jugular again. It may not be as bad this time since most of their blood is currently being redistributed to other areas of their body." I took a different approach.

"No one here is a Swinger, are they?" I asked.

That got their attention, and the whole crowd cheered. They hooted and hollered like only a horny crowd of middle-aged, naked, white people could. I proceeded to do my Swinger material to laughter. No one got offended or approached me afterwards about being disrespectful; they were all too busy rubbing up on one another like a bunch of out-of-shape, wrinkled teenagers.

After that whole experience, I didn't blink an eye last summer when I was asked to play a nudist community. This was different than a nudist resort. At the time of booking it, I really wasn't concerned about the difference between a nudist resort and a nudist community. It was a paid gig, plus I had the extra bonus of all of the comedians in the line-up being friends of mine. I figured the details would work themselves out.

When I attended the gig, the differences were glaringly obvious. The previous clothing-optional resort was a beautiful area filled with well-groomed foliage, lawns, and gorgeous buildings. This particular nudist community was an RV and trailer park that naked people lived in. The attractiveness level of the people was the same, but the surroundings weren't nearly as pretty.

Other differences were just as obvious to me. This community didn't have the "towel rule." No towels--just bare butts, coochies, and nut sacks sitting everywhere their hearts desired, on the bar stools, chairs, benches, any place that one could sit, with snail trails anywhere and everywhere. The beautiful bar with a stage that the resort had was replaced by a screened-in lanai called The Butt Hut. Fun fact: This gig took place in August, in Florida.

Most of the people here were fully nude, not just partially clothed. One general rule I've found from just observing groups of naked people milling about: It is the smaller, finer-built men who are the larger endowed of the male species. The really big guys, 6'-plus types, were all sporting sleeping moles, while the smaller guys, maybe 5'8" to 5'11", had their manhood swinging back and forth like pendulums on a Grandfather clock.

I had also noticed that the people here were a lot friendlier. In fact, most were downright hospitable and neighborly. They all wanted to talk to the comedians. They thanked us for coming out and providing a show for them. They were really wonderful, salt-of-the-earth type people. It was just hard to know where to look while having a conversation with them.

When it came time to do my actual set here, I decided to open up with my same no-clothes-on standard: "I hear you guys would give the shirts off your backs for a good comedy show." This crowd then proceeded to cheer for me to take off my shirt. I have never been the exhibitionist type. Even back in my crazy twenties, I never flashed my breasts for beads or mooned people in passing cars. I don't know if it is vanity or lack of confidence, but public nudity has really never been my thing. So I spent at least the next three minutes explaining to tables full of people--both women and men--that I was, in fact, going to keep my shirt on for the duration of my set.

"I am not taking off my shirt. That is not who I am," I told them.

"Come on, take it off," the crowd cheered back.

"No, seriously, I am not taking my fucking top off, people!"

I finally continued with my act, staying fully clothed. They were attentive and fun and laughed at my jokes. That is all any comedian really wants from a crowd. It was a great night. All in all, they were a wonderful, caring, fun group of (naked) people.

I look at these kinds of gigs like I used to look at traveling outside the United States. It was a cultural unfamiliar to me. I wouldn't want to live there, but visiting gives me an appreciation for what I have. In this case, it is appreciation for not ever knowing what my neighbors look like in the buff.

Chapter Three
The Road Less Groveled

In Tampa, there are only two big comedy clubs. In the comedy world, the clubs that have several shows throughout the week and bigger named headliners on the weekends are considered "A" rooms. The "B" and "C" rooms are comedy clubs that may be something else during the week, like a restaurant, bar or a bowling alley. They mainly feature regional headliners. Then there are "one-nighters." These are bars or pubs that have an occasional "Comedy Night." It may be a once a week show, or a once a month show. It is generally local talent that works "one-nighters," unless the room has a decent budget to pay a well-known headliner.

As a newer comedian, "B" and "C" rooms are easier to be a part of. You meet the comedians who are on their way up or on their way down, and some who have just hit a plateau at being regional comics. As a comedian, especially a new one, you should seek out stage time wherever you can get it. You will find the stage time in clubs, bars, coffee houses, and any open mic that will have you. There should be no snobbery when it comes to stages. You want to make sure that when you get seen in an "A" room, you have brought your best game.

"A" rooms are awesome. You get to perform on stages where people are actually listening to you and came to see comedy. Most good "A" rooms don't tolerate hecklers or "comedy helpers"—people who constantly contribute to your set from their seat. A really good room will even boot out people who are being loud at their table. I don't get to play the "A" rooms that often, but when I do, it's fantastic.

If a club knows how to market itself well, it will always have a full house. Often the "A" clubs will "paper the room." This is when they give tickets away. The real money in comedy is in the booze. You have a built-in audience for 90 minutes, with nothing to do but keep bending their elbows until the show is over. As hacky and cliché as it is, "the drunker you are, the funnier we get," is very true. Also, the more money that can be made from comedy, they more comedy you will see.

It's my observation that papering the room, or reducing the ticket prices, is really the best way to get people out to the club, especially on an "off" night. It is a win-win, especially in a recession. The crowd feels like they are getting something for free, the owners make a ton of cash on the always overpriced two-item minimum, and the and the comics enjoy being seen by a big crowd, getting their name out in hopes people will remember them and their following will grow. It's the circle of comedy life. Side note: The comics' cut of the money is always the smallest amount. In exact terms, the headliner gets paid the most, the feature barely gets paid, the emcee works for peanuts, and the guest sets are always unpaid. Comedy isn't a get-rich-quick-industry for the comedians, but if you have the stand up passion within you, the stage time is its own reward.

There is an exception to this last rule, and it comes into play when there is a headliner who is well-known or already has a following. In this case, people will pay money to see the headliner. There are a lot of funny headlining comedians out there who aren't well known or may not have a big draw. Why would someone want to go see a comedian that they have never heard of and shell out money for a two-drink minimum, when they can stay home and be entertained at their house via TV, video games, and computer? Modern-day entertainment has a lot of options for which you don't even have to leave the house. Many people don't agree with me, but until a comedian hits household-name status, something has to give to keep live comedy going. The ticket prices are that something.

Early in my career, I did a guest set at a Thursday show in an "A" room. This room doesn't have a traditional "Open Mic Night"; rather, they just have comedians do a few minutes of time on an off-night show. This arrangement works well. The new comics are getting to play to a real crowd, the club sees the fresh local talent, and the real comics look that much funnier if the open mic-ers don't do well. The headliner on this particular night was very funny, but not famous, so the club papered the room. It was absolutely jam-packed. At first I was sitting at a little table off to the side where the open mic-ers usually sat, and then the club kicked me out of my seat for "real" customers. I then sat smashed at a table with other open mic-ers, but before long the wait staff had the comics stand as to give every available table to the patrons.

This is in contrast to some smaller comedy rooms that I have played. They don't advertise, they don't market, and sometimes they can't scrape six people together on a Saturday 8:00 show. Often the bookers of the "B" and "C" rooms are bringing the comedy to a venue. They only get to keep the money made from tickets, minus what they pay the comics, so they aren't going to GIVE anything away. The venue keeps the food and drink money, and the guy who gets to keep the booze money always wins.

When you work in an "A" room, you get to work with established headliners, comedians who have spent decades perfecting their act. Sometimes when you work only the local market, you get a false sense of how well you are doing. You may absolutely kill in comparison to the other people you share a stage with in a local show. Working with the pros humbles you; it shows you how much higher you can go and how much harder you need to work to get there. Those awesome "A"-room gigs don't come easily, at least not for me. I had been performing comedy for five years before I was hired as an emcee for a local "A" club. I only work that room occasionally, but I have had some of my best experiences of my career there. It has been a privilege to work with some amazing headliners. Thus far I have hosted for a few quasi-well known people. I have worked with a former soap opera star, a former sitcom cast member, and a nationally known radio DJ singer, to name a few.

One of my most memorable nights was when I got to emcee for the soap actor. I am not going to mention him by name, as I haven't really researched the legalities of name-dropping and his is only one of the few names I can drop. I originally asked the club if I could emcee for him, as I had watched that soap that since I was eight years old and would have loved to meet him. The club told me "no" at the time, but I was offered the gig later. I found out that the original emcee had turned them down.

Sloppy seconds, I will take them. Hell, I will take thrift-shop thirds or falling-apart fourths; I really don't care, just as long I can be under that hot spotlight.

On the day of the show, I got a message from the club asking me if I would pick up the soap actor at his hotel. What? I said yes immediately, but then, like almost every decision that I make, I regretted it instantly. I have two vehicles. They are both paid for because I have had them for a long time. Neither is in great condition. My choices were either picking up a soap star in a shitty, squeaky Ford Explorer or a less shitty Ford Freestyle that my children treat like their personal garbage can. I chose the Explorer. I could clean up the Explorer and have it look halfway presentable. The Freestyle has stains that no amount of car cleaner could ever permeate. If the interior of that car were a person, it would need years of therapy to deal with the abuse and torture my children have put it through.

When I picked up the soap opera actor, he was nothing like the character he played. I knew logically he wasn't the same guy, but I guess I assumed he would kind of be like the suave character that he portrayed. In "real life," he was very nice and a cool guy. He was also a chain smoker who cursed quite a bit for the duration of the ride. Not that it offended me. I just wasn't expecting it from the well-coiffed, dapper character he had portrayed for years on television. He had been in my car for all of three minutes when my anxiety immediately went out the window. He was just a regular guy, trying to feed his family by hustling laughs. He was no different from me or any other person who has been bitten by the comedy bug.

The sitcom actor whom I worked with was a great guy as well. I was a bigger fan of the soap opera than of the sitcom, so I wasn't as star-struck. He was a joy to be around, just down to earth and funny both on and off stage. Again, I was in charge of giving him a ride to the club every night. Those are the times when you are sitting at a red light making small talk with someone that you have seen for years on TV and think, "This is my life, really? That guy is in my car, right now."

My husband, Joe, was absolutely star struck when he knew I would be working with the sitcom actor. I arranged to have my neighbors watch the kids for a couple of hours so Joe could come with me to one of the early shows. Joe and I picked up the sitcom star. This was a Saturday, and I had worked with the actor on Thursday and Friday. He and I were casually chatting about comedy. My husband was starry-eyed and would randomly quote some of the lines from the sitcom the actor had been on. At one point the actor asked if we could stop by Starbucks, so he could get some coffee. We parked, and the actor walked into the building. When he came back and sat back down in the passenger seat next to my husband, Joe squeezed his shoulder and said "I am so sorry I just have to touch you. I can't really believe I am this close to you."

It was a very sweet moment. Later that night, the actor called my husband onto the stage. He always incorporated audience members in his act, and he gave Joe a good-natured ribbing in front of the audience. My husband loved it and always looks back fondly on that evening.

I worked a weekend at that same "A" club with woman headliner whom I really admired. She is a great example of a fantastic comedian who isn't a household name. As a comedian and a comedy nerd, I knew who she was and was thrilled to share a stage with her. She has been in the business for twenty-plus years. Her act was clean and about her kids and family life. She killed show after show. She is who I want to be, but I don't know how to achieve her brand of humor going through the amateur ranks. I had plenty of material involving my kids and personal stories that weren't traditional jokes. I had also experienced bombing on my butt to certain audiences when I tried them. If I was at a bar or if the audience was full of younger people, no one wanted to hear about a middle-aged mom and her wacky take on life. Yet, here was this seasoned headliner standing in an "A" room, ripping the roof off of the place for four consecutive nights. To me, it was like watching the Olympic snow skiers who do flips in the air after hurling themselves off a steep ramp. If you can do it right, it is awesome and impressive, but how in God's name do you actually practice it without killing yourself?

The problem with the big rooms, though, is that everyone wants to be a part of them. The entire local comedy scene clamors to play them. Every club has people they predominately use. Every club has its own cliques. It is like high school all over again, except in high school, you know there will eventually be an end date. In comedy, this IS the real world. There is no graduation ceremony. You have to either play by the clubs' rules or make your own.

I have taken my career into my own hands, kind of. I had a once-a-month room that I ran, booked and emceed on the second Saturday of every month. The Pursuit Pub was a bar on the other 29 or 30 days of the month, but for the one evening, I turned it into a comedy club--a loud, sometimes distracted, but always memorable comedy club. The Pursuit Pub had tried a comedy night prior to my running the show. It had been run the way many local comedy shows are run, with a lineup of 10 to 12 comics who all performed for five to seven minutes. It started late and was a long show. The next month, the show had many of the same comics doing the same jokes. By the time the third show came around, it was still some of the very same comics telling the same jokes that had been told for the third consecutive month. The fourth and very last show started an hour and a half late, the crowd was loud, the comics got mad that they couldn't be heard, and the drunken patrons started heckling. It almost turned into a fist fight.

The bar didn't want to have comedy again after that debacle, but I couldn't let the Comedy Night die in that place. The owner of the bar, Tab, had gone to great lengths to hand-paint a brick wall background on a pull-down screen. At the first show, the stage was literally a couple of crates tied together. By the time the fourth show rolled around, Tab had constructed a big portable stage that could be created and subsequently retracted in minutes. I felt like all the effort that had gone into the Comedy Nights at the bar couldn't be discarded so easily, even though I worried about the politics of taking over a room that had some bad comedy mojo attached to it. The thought of the stage and the fake brick wall haunted me in my sleep. "Those items shouldn't be collecting dust in someone's garage," I mused to myself. "They need to live comedy life the way it was meant to be lived in a bar room, hit or miss."

I decided that if I were to take over the room, I wouldn't make it a showcase show, which is where you have a lot of comics doing small amount of time. The real comedy clubs and successful one-nighters always have a three-person lineup, the emcee, the feature, and the headliner. Some shows may have a guest set spot or two. The guest spots are usually comics who are just starting out and do five to six minutes, while the feature does 25 to 30 minutes and the headliner does a regular 45-minute set. I felt the best way to pay the comics was to get a flat rate from the bar, rather than to charge an admission price. Offer comedy for free, charge the bar a set entertainment fee and again, the crowd would drink for 90 uninterrupted minutes. I figured, "Bars pay other entertainers, like bands or the trivia people. Why can't they pay for comics?" I didn't ask for a lot of money. I would pay myself for booking and emceeing the shows, which would also give me guaranteed monthly stage times, and I would pay the feature and the headliner. The only non-paying spot would be a guest set.

I approached The Pursuit Pub about possibly bringing back the monthly comedy show. I met with Tab and his bar manager. I borrowed from my past life when I worked in corporate America and came in with a written proposal. I think they were a little taken aback. I outlined everything that I wanted from them and exactly what I could give them in return. I even included limiting the number of comped drinks per comic. I wanted them to know that I was serious and on the up- and-up. I had Tab talked into it right away. The manager was a different story. She had not been in the least bit amused by the antics at the last show. I had to convince them that I would bring in different comics every month. I promised to never repeat the same headliners in a 12-month time frame, so the crowd would see a fresh act at every show. In return, I asked them to turn off the televisions when the comics were on stage. That one I lost. They agreed to turn off all the televisions set except for the one at the very back of the bar.

That back television was one of the biggest challenges. The Pursuit Pub doesn't serve food, and in Florida, if a bar makes less than 10 percent of its revenue from food, people can smoke at that location. So a lot of people will go there to watch whatever big game is on, drink, and have a smoke with their friends. The owner was worried that if I were to turn off every television, the regulars would walk out. The comedy nights had to compete with hockey playoffs, football playoffs, World Series games, and NASCAR races; if it is a captivating sport on the second Saturday of the month, it's a force to be reckoned with.

A real comedy club would never in a million years have anything competing for the audience's attention, but this wasn't a real club; it was a place that gave me a shot at running my own show. I also had to tread lightly on how I handle noisy crowds; hecklers can be taken of care by the comics. If someone starts up with a comic for the sake of being an asshole, then they get what is coming to them; with most good bar comics, a heckler doesn't really stand a chance. The "Chatty Cathys" are different. They are the people who talk for the entire duration of the show. I couldn't tell a regular patron of the bar to shut up or leave; that would have gotten me and my show kicked out. I would "shush" them, and occasionally it worked, but most of the time it didn't. Sometimes I felt as if I was doing the comics and comedy in general a disservice when a show went really awry at my club, but then again, I had had bad shows at other bars and never took it to be anything more than just another insane night of doing comedy.

Booking a room helped me understand why some bookers act the way they do. Bookers can be perceived as assholes. Some never return calls, emails, texts, carrier pigeon messages…nothing. It really is a case of supply and demand, though. There are a bazillion local comedians and only one bar that I booked. I could only hire 12 features and 12 headliners per year, but I got tons of requests from comics from the Tampa and Orlando area. I was occasionally contacted by out-of-state comics as well, to work the room.

There have been some memorable experiences in that room that will probably always stick with me. I wanted the first few shows to really knock both the audience's and management's socks off. I was able to book an incredibly funny and talented comedian to headline my second show. "Cousin Mo" was local to the area, but had been in comedy for decades and had performed all over the world. He was more than just a comedian. He was a wonderful musician as well. His act consisted of him singing and playing both the guitar and banjo. He also took straight music gigs when he wasn't performing comedy.

He did phenomenally that night. The crowd loved him, including Tab. Later, I found out through the grapevine (Facebook) that Tab hired "Cousin Mo" to play music there on a week night. I didn't think much of it. Mo was an entertainer and got hired quite a bit. I learned that during his music gig, the crowd was trying to get him to do his comedy act, but he refused. Mo told them that I booked comedy there and he didn't feel right since this was booked as a music gig. The rest of the night, he played his music and didn't perform any comedy out of loyalty to me. It touched me so much that he had been in the business for years, but treated me like a peer. Cousin Mo passed away the next year. I will always remember the professionalism and respect that he showed me.

There was another show with a headliner I had hired who later died. That show was wild. The crowd was particularly rambunctious. The front half of the room was attentive, but the back half got loud, and their noise started to dominate the room. The guest set went all right, but the feature had to compete with the noise, which was getting louder and louder. When the headliner, "Bart," got up, he had to deal with the noise plus two hecklers at the bar. At a certain point, Bart got off the stage with the microphone in hand and confronted the hecklers. It was a weird moment, but the hecklers left, and Bart tried to salvage what was left of his set. The commotion got everyone's attention, and as he continued, the back half of the room became loud again. It is always at this point in the night that I drink more. I can't toss the patrons out of the bar, as it is not my bar, but I am responsible for bringing the comics. I hate throwing the comedians into the lion's den, and there is only so much "shushing" with a stern face I can do. The patrons are grown (drunk) adults. They are going to do what they want.

Bart started to tell a midget joke. It was a clever joke--not particularly derogatory to little people, as Bart was a fantastic joke writer, but he did use the word "midget." Midway through his bit, I saw a blur rush past me. A real-life little person charged the stage. "Who you calling a midget?" she yelled. Her tiny little legs were hauling ass. The place went nuts. No one really knew what to do. I got so busy trying to run the show and making sure the comedians were doing okay that I didn't always pay that much attention to the patrons. The little-person lady had been in the back of the room for awhile, as it turned out. The headliner was dumfounded. He stepped down from the stage and gave her a hug. People were cheering and taking pictures. She went back to the bar, and Bart finished his set. It was one of the most unforgettable evenings, and a memory that I hold dear when I think about my friend, Bart.

Things moved along at the room, until I got a call on a random Wednesday morning while I was running. Some woman was on the other end of the phone. She sounded like she had smoked 10,000 cigarettes in her lifetime. In a deep, raspy voice, she told me that she had taken over the management of The Pursuit Pub and officially shit-canned me in that phone conversation. I had known running a room would someday come to an end. I was just a little disappointed that it had ended in such a detached way—that the owners of The Pursuit Pub had sent a lackey to do the dirty work for them. I really wasn't upset that it ended, but was disappointed by the lack of respect I was shown. It felt like the equivalent of being in a rocky three-year relationship and getting dumped, by phone, by the other person's out-of-town aunt, who had smoked 10,000 Marlboro Reds the night before.

Sometimes, the future of my comedy career seems so bright. Sometimes I have nothing on my calendar for weeks on end and feel like a complete failure. I want to be the comedy superstar and have the HBO specials, but overall I just want to continue to take the stage and make people laugh. I occasionally ask myself, "If being a local comic is all I will ever be, would I be happy?" Then I think back to the people I have met, and the places I have been, and the weird nights that came along with pursuing this dream—and I wouldn't change a thing.

Chapter Four
Stand Up and Be a Lady

In the world of stand up comedy, all men may be created equal, but that rule doesn't apply to women. It is still very much a man's world. Countless times, audience members have come up to me after a show and said, "I usually don't like female comics, but you were pretty funny." Most clubs will have weekend after weekend of male-dominated shows. I have been turned down for work or had gigs changed if another woman comic performs on the same bill because the club did not want to have more than one woman in the line-up. And, if a club does have more than one female comic scheduled, the whole thing is often labeled, "Ladies Night."

This is kind of crazy to me. There is no "Men's Night" in comedy. Men, especially young men, will joke about their dick, telling not just one joke, but joke after joke after joke. It isn't specialty or niche comedy; it is standard in the industry. But a woman has a laundry list of topics that she is not supposed to talk about and jokes she is not supposed to tell, because they are considered "hack" or stereotypical. Included on this list are: coochy jokes, period jokes (including jokes about tampons or maxi- pads), jokes about being under-/over-sexed, and "bitches" about kids and/or husbands.

Woman in comedy also had its share of famous critics. Jerry Lewis recently restated his disdain for women comics. He said that he hated to see women perform comedy and diminish themselves for the lowest common dominator. I guess a guy who spent his career contorting his face and playing the stooge to Dean Martin's straight man would find comedy to be diminishing. That's not my definition of comedy or the intent of comedy for all comedians.

George Carlin, for one, didn't diminish himself through comedy or cater to the lowest common dominator. He used comedy to show society its own hypocrisies and absurdities. Richard Pryor used comedy to show his vulnerabilities and human flaws, all while bringing stadiums of people to their knees with laughter using his personal stories. Bob Newhart, Ellen DeGeneres, and Steven Wright have all been cerebral comics that used words as their wit, not pratfalls. So I was almost more offended by Jerry Lewis' "diminishing statement" about comedy than by what he said about women in comedy.

What I do find interesting is how the whole debate over women being funny has been accepted by the masses. There has never been a huge outrage. Instead, it is accepted as a topic to be debated by the masses. Had Jerry Lewis made those comments about any other group based on ethnicity or sexual preference, it would have been disputed. He would have been ostracized, but since it was about women being funny, people spoke of the pros and cons as if it were a great debate for the ages.

As much as I disagree with the whole argument, a part of me feels that protesting that women are indeed funny does not convince anyone otherwise. I feel that it is almost like adding oxygen to a flame. All I can do is continue to do what I have been doing—writing jokes, going on stage, and working on my craft. In the meantime, I look to "established" funny women for inspiration—those on whose shoulders all comedians, male and female alike are standing on. I'm talking icons like Carol Burnett, Phyllis Diller, and Lucille Ball, along with the more modern Tina Fey, Amy Poehler, and Chelsea Handler.

I am really not sure why there is a stigma about women in comedy. I found a lot of women to be funny prior to ever hearing that women weren't supposed to be funny. I remember, as a kid, watching the "Carol Burnett Show" religiously. My entire family would all crack up at the skits each week—my very serious, former-Marine father included. In fact, I remember hating the musical breaks in the show. To me, that was the boring part, and I wanted them to go back to the funny skits. I also distinctly remember watching Gilda Radner play Rosanne Rosanna Dana for the first time on "Saturday Night Live." My brother and I laughed so hard we could barely breathe. The look of her character, the hair, her diatribes, and the cadence of everything she said were unbelievably hilarious to me. This was back before VCRs. My brother and I used to tape the audio with a cassette tape recorder and play it back. We would laugh just as hard listening to it replayed as when we had watched it live.

Even in my own family, women were funny. It was my mother who told my brother and me jokes. Every Helen Keller joke I know was told to me by my Mom. I remember her telling me the joke about the handicapped kid who would only get an ice cream cone if he could clap three times. She would do a belabored impression of a spastic little kid trying desperately to put his hands together three consecutive times, and then, when the treat was given to him, he inadvertently smashed it on his forehead instead of eating it because he was too spastic to put it in his mouth. That was funny AND good parenting, all in one.

Despite all the stigma, being a woman in comedy has also led to a lot of experiences that I would never have had in any other realm or universe. I often feel like being a comedian makes me a superhero of sorts—though not one who fights crime, helps the community, or saves anybody from danger. It lets me remain that crazy, young invincible person that I once thought I put away years ago. Yeah, during most of the week, I have to be a Mom and try to act like a grown-up. I help the kids with homework, make lunches in the morning, and drudge through the car line Monday through Friday. But on gig weekends, I find that the crazy bitch inside of me, the one whose existence would make my mother weep if she was aware of it, that same person that I pray my daughter will never become—yeah, her—she comes back every now and again and reminds me of who I really am. When I am on stage, I feel like the person I was in my youth—fun and free.

One of my most unique, "lady-comic" experiences happened very early in my career, as I was emceeing one night at a club. An "open mic-er" I had known from the area came in. (For those unfamiliar with comedy terms, an open mic-er is an amateur comedian who has not yet been paid to perform, and whose only stage time is obtained at an open mic. There are a lot of arguments in the comedy world about at which point you go from being an open mic-er to a comic. I think that if you get paid on a regular basis to do comedy, you have graduated to comedian. Others feel that label doesn't apply until you can support yourself with your craft.) This particular open mic-er told me that he had just dropped his girlfriend off at the airport and rushed to the show in hopes of catching my act. He said he was a big fan; although he did not much like women comics, he thought I had potential. I tried not to take his comments too seriously, as they were coming from someone who was not getting steady weekend work as I was. I remember our exact conversation:

Open Mic-er, "I think you are funny because you are kind of androgynous."

Me: "Excuse me?"

Open Mic-er "Oh, I am sorry. I think I used the wrong term. You have both masculine and feminine qualities."

Me: "No, you used the correct term. That is what 'androgynous' means."

Open Mic-er: "Don't get me wrong. I think you are sexy. You just need to wear clothes that show off your body more. I am always rooting for you when you go on stage. Part of me feels like you are my little sister, and another part of me really wants to fuck you."

Me: "Well, thanks for that feedback."

Open Mic-er "I hope you don't think I am being an asshole. I mean it as a compliment."

Me: "Sure. How could I possibly take it any other way?"

On another night, I was emceeing a weekend gig and the headliner was talking to his feature act about a woman comedian from another city. "She's sexy and she's funny," the headliner said. "That's something you don't see much in a woman comic. They are either one or the other."

The feature agreed and walked away. The headliner then turned to me and said, in a New York accent, "I don't want you to think there is anything wrong with you. Don't do anything stupid, like getting plastic surgery or something like that. You look just fine."

I felt like a Southern Belle in the mid-nineteenth century, waving a giant fan as I said, while batting my eyelashes, "Oh my, 'Just fine.' I do declare, you are making me blush, you kind gentleman."

For a couple of years in my career, I was in an all-female comedy troupe called "The Hilarious Hustlas." We started out as nine women, all of varying backgrounds and different ethnicities and with different levels of experience. Some of us had been in comedy for awhile, some had just started out, and a few had performed stand up earlier in their life and come back to it. None of us, though, were at the point in our career that we were regularly featuring on our own.

When a comedian first starts out, they are at the mercy of open mics. Most open mics only give comics five minutes of time. It takes years to cultivate an act, especially if you are only given a small amount of time to hone your craft. The idea behind the comedy troupe was that we could all give ourselves more time than the allotted 5 minutes at most clubs. It was also that if we could package and market ourselves, maybe we could earn a little money while building our act instead of paying gas and obligatory beverage money in return for performing at open mics or taking non-paid guest sets.

"The Hilarious Hustlas" started when my friend Mary, who had then only been in comedy for a few months, was asked to headline at a local venue, The Ocean Rock Hideaway. It was a cozy little location that looked like a coffee shop—with comfy couches, small round tables, and funky art adorning the walls—but it sold booze, which is a must for comedy audiences. Mary had been gently told by a seasoned comic not to headline so early in her career. Even though new comics in all their enthusiasm feel that they have enough material to jump right into the main role, they usually do not. Mary then decided to take the stage time she had been offered and to start a female group instead.

The Ocean Rock Hideaway ended up being the launching pad for the group. It was home to our first few shows. We did pretty well as a group initially, with nine comics in the line-up. We all got to perform for around 10 minutes each in a real show where the audiences were made up of our friends, family, and OR Hideaway's regulars. This crowd was a lot more fun and attentive than a typical open mic audience. We had a great time first few shows and earned a little bit of money to boot.

Then we decided to expand our horizons from our original venue. I approached a booker, who at the time ran a club in the spare room of a fancy resort in the area. He was not willing to book a group of "newbies" on his regular weekend shows, but he was willing to wheel and deal with us to book a Saturday early show (the regular shows were at 9:00, but he would make exceptions and occasionally book 7:00 shows). His original deal was that the "Hustlas" would have to market and sell the show, with the profits split 70/30. This meant the "Hustlas" would get 70% of the profits, and the club would get

30% of the profits. That was the original deal, but here is what actually happened:

We sold out the show. We had nine women, all of whom tried their best to persuade their friends and family to come out. We bombarded social media with virtual flyers, we littered the streets with paper flyers, and, since it was our show, we negotiated ticket prices. Most of the "Hustlas" gave their friends a two-for-one discount. We were selling a lot of tickets, and we were all very excited.

On the night of the show, it fast became clear that the booker had never told anyone at the resort that there was going to be an early show. Even though the show had been booked for months and the lobby walls were papered with our posters, the connection was never made. Even worse, the booker did not come to the show that night. Instead, he sent his wife to run the "club." I decided to come early and got to witness the wife informing the resort they needed to unlock their comedy room for the line of people that was now starting to form in their lobby.

The manager of the resort was irate. He had to scramble to get waitresses and bartenders to come in early. He had to set up the room and prepare for a big event about which he had never been informed. Normally this type of situation would have made me anxious, but because this miscommunication was no fault of my own, I had peace of mind. Besides, everyone was going to make money from it in the end. The resort, though unprepared, was going to reap the benefits of 90 or so hungry and thirsty patrons coming out to laugh, have a good time, and drink on a Saturday night.

Rather than trying to prepare my set and get in my comedy "head", the booker's wife asked me if I could help her take the tickets and ticket money, some of the other members of the group were seating the audience members. At a later point in the night, the manager of the resort lost his mind a second time when the fire code was violated because we had exceeded the occupancy rate and the restaurant ran out of chicken for the second show, the only show he and his staff had known about ahead of time.

Despite all the chaos before the show, the actual comedy part of the night was fantastic. Everyone had great sets; the adrenaline and craziness of the night just heightened the energy in our performances. I remember being in post-comedy euphoria at the end of the show—which is equivalent to a good set mixed with a couple of Michelob Ultras. All I had to do was get the group's 70 percent of the take, and we could put a cork in the night.

I went to the booker's wife to count out the money, and that was when my happiness was washed away by the dirty politics of dealing with dirty bookers. She had counted out the money, and stated that she had calculated the number of tickets sold times the face value of the tickets minus the sales by credit card purchases made that night (they had no way of splitting the credit card money that night, since there were transactions costs involved and it took several days for them to get the funds from the credit companies) She informed me that she was going to give us 70 percent of that total.

"You have got to be fucking kidding me???" I said. "That was not the original agreement that I made with your husband. He said 70/30, period. He didn't talk about any fancy comedy math, or credit card machines, or the value of a ticket for a show that wouldn't have existed otherwise. Half of these tickets were sold at two-for-one. We wouldn't have agreed to that had we known."

"He is always so bad at explaining that to people," the woman said, throwing her husband under the bus.

I was absolutely livid at this point. "This is bullshit!" I shouted. "We have to figure out something else. You wouldn't have made a dime had it not been for us. It was family, friends and neighbors of the girls in the group that made up the audience. I am not going back to them looking like a jack-ass while you guys pocket the money on a show that you totally dropped the ball on!"

At that point, the wife knew I was not going to walk away from this situation. She said that she would call her husband and see what they could do. As it turned out, the credit card sales for that night had equaled roughly 30% of the total ticket sales. I told them to take the credit card money, but the cash was rightfully ours. After a year, the resort's owners, who had had enough of the "comedy club" and all the antics that came with it, stopped having comedy nights there.

That was the first of many shows at many venues that we performed in those few years, and we learned a valuable lesson about whom to book with and whom to trust. As time went by, the group dwindled down to just four of us. We would take advantage of the "Ladies Night Out" mentality of all-women comedy shows. That was how we billed ourselves. Even as the group thinned down, we still had a variety in the lineup. Two of us, me included, were pretty clean. The other two were a bit bawdier. It did work. We treated our audiences to a little bit of everything, including jokes about family, kids, marriage, relationships, and sex, plus any other miscellaneous content that we had in our arsenal.

It was sometimes hard to work and function as a group. Traditionally, you do not get paid a lot in comedy. We would score gigs, but we would always have to split the pay four ways. Although we were all different, the longer we worked together, the more it seemed that our jokes tended to meld with other members' jokes. Sometimes we would have to refrain from doing certain jokes because they sounded too much like someone else's. There was also a competitive element to it. I always remembered each show and who had performed best that night. It would vary from show to show and crowd to crowd, and it was never spoken aloud, but we all kept score.

I learned a lot about myself from this whole group experience. The first lesson was that I really do not work well in groups. I fancy myself a pretty laid-back person, but I may just fancy myself a bit too much. In hindsight, I was a pretty big jerk at times. I always wanted to be the one who did the best. I would get irritated when a show became awkward because one of the members struggled on stage and even more irritated when I was the one who was struggling.

Also, as time went on the more shows we did, the more material we had and the better we all became. It got to a point where we were all starting to get booked individually rather than just as a group, which for me was the whole reason for being in the group in the first place. Finally, I had to be honest and accept that it was time to move on. I had to accept that I did not become a comedian to be a team player, to work together, and to build a product. I became a comedian so I could stand alone under the hot, white lights, and have people laugh at my words, my jokes, and my slice of life. I do not want to have shared glory; I do not want to be a member in a band. I want to be the rock star. My only regret is having learned this only after having spent two years with three other people, trying to make it work.

I do have some great memories from being in that troupe, and I still maintain friendships and professional relationships with the other women. We had a buzz about us for awhile. We had a string of sold-out shows. We were riding high for a time. I have boxes full of old flyers and pictures of our past shows. We had a tradition of going to Chili's after every show. Some of those post-show meals were more fun and laughter-filled than the show itself. When I am elderly and look back, I hope it is those memories that will stick out in my mind.

Chapter Five
Please Don't Repeat This

When I was in my late teens and early twenties, I loved to drink, socialize and act like a buffoon. I went to a lot of parties and bars, where a band was sometimes part of the night's entertainment. I like music, but I prefer the way the music industry delivers it—in small, three- to four-minute increments—over the way it is delivered at live music events, where musicians play longer versions of songs you may hear on the radio or just really long songs you may never have heard of. At some point during these events, a guitar player would inevitably perform a solo that went on for what seemed like an eternity. The longer the riff, the more people would cheer. If the guitar player held a note for a long time, the crowd would cheer even louder. Call me musically uncouth, but I prefer the lyrics to a song. The instrumental part was—and still is—when I tune out.

Of course, I was usually drunk at these dive bars and jam session listening fests. I am not sure if drinking made the experience better or worse, or what it does to that experience now. When the guitar solo comes on, there was just no escape. The music was always way too loud to have any kind of side conversations, so you are stuck feigning interest while everyone else around you is embodying the spirit of the riff by closing their eyes or swaying to the music. At least when you are listening to someone sing, it is a distraction from the permanent damage that is being done to your ears. Some of the people listening play along on their invisible air guitars. The really messed-up spectators just watch intensely, nodding their head to the beat of the song, and will occasionally yell, "Fuck, yeah!"

"Oh god, please stop," I pray when this happens "It is just encouraging them to play even longer."

It's not that I don't have empathy for guitar players. A solo is really a guitar player's only time to shine. They spend most of the gig acting as the lead singer's wingman. I am sure that they are always longing for their day in the sun. I just don't want to hear it. I get it. You know how to play the guitar well, and you can hold a note for a long time. Can we just get back to the lyrics and maybe turn the volume down a smidge?

I am not saying that one's ability to play a guitar isn't impressive. Playing an instrument and playing it well is an admirable talent. It thrills loads of people and inspires others to become guitar players themselves. There are many guitar players whose guitar-playing talent has made them famous: Richie Sambora, Keith Richards, and the master of all guitar riffers, the great Jimi Hendrix. Hendrix was able to make his guitar almost sing—again, insanely impressive, but something that I admire in theory, and not something I want to listen to for an entire evening while tired, bloated and half in the bag.

But guitar-playing isn't the only prolonged art form for which I have no appreciation. I can't tell you how many times I have been bored while watching a car chase scene in an action flick. Unfortunately, I am usually sober when I am watching a movie, which makes it worse since initially my mind will try to follow the contrived plot that justifies the characters pursuing one another in fast vehicles. If I am at home and have been talked into watching one of these movies, I will fall asleep on the couch, waking up every so often when the volume increases dramatically as the "good" parts of the movie flash on the screen.

"Turn that shit down," I will say to my husband.

"Why don't you just go to bed?" he always retorts. "You aren't even watching it anyway. You ruin everything."

Like anything else in life, I realize action movies aren't for everyone. I do not begrudge this genre of film. Hollywood has spent billions of dollars to perfect the chase scene. They pay stunt men, pyrotechnical specialists, and computer-generated Image experts to trump the last car chase scene and make new, improved chase scenes. Audiences will go to the theaters in droves to see these films. You can't get more American than adding money to the economy in the name of being "totally kick-ass." Again, I just don't want to take part in it. I am always amazed that people can get so sucked into car chases scenes with jaws dropped and eyes glued to the screen. Later, they will talk about it: "Did you see that last chase, when the car was on fire and they made that big jump, like 50 feet up in the air? Then they got chased into a dead end street and there was no other way to go, so they turned around and then the car went on only two wheels. That was awesome!"

No, it wasn't. It was six minutes of my life watching the vehicular version of the kids' game "tag."

Recently, tragedy struck the world of car chase enthusiasts with the death of Paul Walker. I truly thought it was sad. Anytime a young, vibrant person loses his life, it is tragic. But because I seldom watch that genre of movies, it took me until I saw the trailer for "The Fast and Furious 3" to realize that Paul Walker was not the same guy who played Zack in the television show "Saved by the Bell." Although if anyone from that show should become a regular star of car chase movies, Dustin Diamond is the one. Screech.

I think the reason I personally have zero desire to watch these movies is that I have cracked the car chase code. If it is the beginning or middle of the movie, the bad guy wins the car chase. If it is the end of the movie, the good guys win the car chase. That is it. It is every movie plot that includes a car chase. The equivalent here is the end of every chick flick movie, where the guy and girl kiss in the pouring rain. I knew it would happen. You knew what would happen. There was really no other way to end it. Kissing on an overcast day or indoors isn't as sexy as being soaking wet. The only exception to this "kissing rule" is when the final scene of the movie is set at an airport and one of the star-crossed lovers is leaving "forever" to go to another country.

Even real car chases don't interest me. Sometimes, actual live police pursuits are televised on CNN. The cops and state troopers have the helicopters and a zillion squad cars trying to capture someone who is attempting to escape arrest. Granted, the real-life car chases are more captivating than movie car chases, but I am usually worried that some innocent bystander will get hurt. It is a lot of anxiety for me. At some point, I will turn off the television and promise myself to follow up on the outcome that evening in the news or Google it to see the how it turned out later that day. Who needs that kind of stress?

The repetitive nature of horror movies makes them equally less than compelling to me. I haven't watched a scary movie in literally decades, because doing it is like getting a hickey, drinking Boons Farm wine or wearing short skirts—things I have deemed no longer appropriate for someone my age. In every horror movie plot, there seems to be a time when maybe the good guy could win, but alas, scary shit keeps happening until the very end. Nothing is ever truly resolved, especially in the franchise movies, like the "Nightmare on Elm Street" and "Friday the 13th" films. No matter how many times they kill the bad guy in the earlier movies, he somehow comes back in the later ones. The reasoning never has to be that rock-solid, either. If you ask me, it is simply that people who love the horror genre of films are just ecstatic to have their favorite serial killer back again and ready to slaughter!

I feel the same way about street jokes—those long jokes people may tell at a party or tavern. There is a difference between a stand up comedian who writes and performs his or her own material and a guy who can repeat a joke that has been told to him. Having a mental rolodex of street jokes and the ability to recite them anytime they get wasted around friends doesn't make a person a comedian. It makes them a drunk who tells street jokes. I find this form of joke-telling to be yet another painstakingly repetitive event in which I am always reluctant to participate.

There is an unwritten (and erroneous) perception that the longer a street joke takes to tell, the funnier it is. When a bunch of friends are sitting around telling jokes, the set-up is retold over and over again. I guess the (wrong) logic is that if the punch line is prolonged, it makes the joke funnier—like some sort of tantric comedy. It does not work, at least not for me. In a world of YouTube, Vine videos, and Internet memes, comedy is quick. No one has the attention span to hear long setups repeated a hundred times. If you tell me a joke that takes three minutes to get to the punch line, that punch line needs to come with cash, or a "happy ending," or a gift certificate to my favorite restaurant—something to compensate for my time lost on listening to you ramble.

Still, when some people discover you're a comedian, they are compelled to tell you a street joke. It usually comes from a straight-laced guy with a secret desire to be a comedian. He never tried to go on stage. He prefers to be the guy who tells the jokes at the bar. He is the same guy who comes to you with a twinkle in his eye and a proud smile, and says, "I got one for you. It is a good one." He will look you right in the eye, even when you try to break the gaze. He cannot wait to see your reaction. So it is always a mental toss up….Do you fake a laugh when the punch line FINALLY comes? If so, you risk hearing his other jokes, as he will take your laughter as positive reinforcement. Or do you watch his proud smile fade if you cut him off and say, "Oh yeah… I have heard that one…many times." (Sometimes, after a prolonged, endless joke, these street joke-tellers will say, "You can use that one on stage if you want!" No, I can't—and even if I could, I don't want to. It was a terrible joke. It was a joke I heard years ago. It was one joke, you took three-and-a- half minutes to tell and I have no cash or Applebee's gift card for my time wasted.

Some comedians will tell street jokes in their act. They will give a disclaimer: "This is a street joke." I am not a fan of that. I think it is cheating of sorts. You don't go to a P!nk concert to hear her sing the "Happy Birthday" song or "Old McDonald Had a Farm", so why would you pay money to go to a club to hear a bar joke? Although I do have to give credit to comics who admit they are telling a street joke, my biggest pet peeve is when a comedian disguises a street joke as real material: "My friend and I were driving down an old dirt road when our car died. We stopped in at this old farm house. The farmer answered the door with his gorgeous daughter. You can sleep in my barn, but keep away from my daughter...." No, that did not happen. Nor did you walk into a bar with a priest and a Rabbi. You also never had a parrot that caught your wife cheating. It is a badly camouflaged street joke. As with bad cheese, I can smell one from a mile away.

I recently made my obligatory once-a-year visit to church. It was on Christmas Eve. I take my children to the evening services in hopes that when they become adults, they will take their children to church once a year as well. As the kids grow older, the only selling point of the evening is the Christmas candlelight service. When they were little, they just got glow sticks, but this year, they were handed candles as we walked in. I agreed to let them hold the candles as long as they behaved themselves when the flame was lit. No fighting or grabbing the other's candle. I was leery of the church giving tiny torches to the children, but honestly a fire in my shaky hands was equally hazardous.

That night, the Pastor used the same technique as people who tell street jokes. He repeated and repeated and repeated the hook of his speech. He was telling a story about why it took God so long to send Jesus to the earth. He literally treated us to five or six minutes of: "Man was evil and asked 'Will you help us God?' And God replied, 'Not yet.' Man didn't listen to God, and man suffered more. Again, Man asked 'Will you help us, God?' and again God replied 'Not yet.' Man continued to sin and be evil, and again man asked 'Will you help us, God?' Again God replied 'Not yet.' Years passed, still man sinned and suffered. They asked God, 'Will you help us now? Again God replied 'Not yet.'"

This went on and on. We got it after the first three "not yets." It took a super-long time for God to send Jesus. We got it. I don't know if the Pastor was stretching out his sermon. Maybe he made it long for dramatic effect. It worked the opposite on me. It annoyed me, and looking over at the glossy-eyed gaze from my two children, I knew this technique was not working on them either. I whispered to them, "You will get to play with fire soon. Hang on."

Anyone who speaks in public should be required to learn the Comedy Rule of Threes. It is the Rule of Threes for a reason: Anything longer than three scenarios is just tedious. Maybe the Pastor was being ironic and was trying to make the congregation suffer the way the people in the Bible had prior to the coming of Jesus. In reality, it made me not want to go back to church on my annual night of going to church.

I guess my intolerance for repetition is part of the reason I am such a comedy nerd. Comedy, not street jokes, is a limitless art form. All too often, people try to jam it into boxes. They ask questions like, "What type of comedian are you? Blue? Insult comic? Clean?

Christian? Redneck?" Comedy can be all of those things or none of them, depending on the comedian.

If an art teacher were to hand out blank canvases to a classroom full of students and told them to draw a flower, none of the flowers would look the same. Some would be bigger than others, some would use multiple colors, some may look like a real flower, and others may be abstract. That is how comedy should be when it comes from the most honest, genuine part of who you are. Whether it's a one-liner, wordplay or just a whimsical observation, it needs to be uniquely from the comedian's point of view, perception of life, personal attitude, essence of their soul and/or outlook on the world...I would continue, but I hate to keep....please pardon the expression....repeating myself.

Chapter Six
My True Disability is My Laziness

Even though I have a neurological condition called Essential Tremor, my real disability is good, old-fashioned laziness. Its symptoms include procrastination, watching too much television, mindless snacking, constantly looking at my smartphone, spending unproductive hours on my computer, daydreaming about what life would be like if I weren't so lazy, and "just chillin." To be honest, being a slothful lump of shit has been more debilitating than my tremor could ever have been—or will ever be. My tremor may have caused me frustration and embarrassment, but laziness has caused me to lose years of my life. Sometimes there is nothing more satisfying than lying on my fat ass for hours on end, doing diddly-squat.

I do have an actual work ethic. I have had a job since I was 15 years old, with the exception of the few years I took off when my children were infants (which was like being on "call" for four straight years, without vacation time, work friends or a salary). When I cared about trying to climb the corporate ladder, I spent more of my waking hours at the office than I did at home. I used to leave the house when it was still dark out and my husband was still asleep. I would come home when it had again turned dark and my husband was napping on the couch. I assumed he went to work between his periods of rest, since the car was sometimes parked at a different angle and his paycheck was always in the bank account every other Friday.

I also had a weird guilt about calling in sick. I would stay home only if I was literally half dead. If I had a hoarse throat or a clogged nose when I called in, I would always feel slightly less guilty, since there was proof that I was sick. If it was a stomach virus, I would generally describe way too many details of my symptoms, to let my bosses and coworkers know that I was legitimately ill. It always made me feel better, but it probably ruined their lunch. So when I talk about being lazy, it is more about laziness that affects me and my own hopes and dreams. When I am on "The Man's" time, I am a perfect worker bee, and when I am my own time, I am a lifeless slug.

Being lazy never elicits much sympathy or support. No one ever has a telethon for lazy people. There is no Foundation for Procrastination. There is also no poster or poster child for lethargy. No lazy person would have the energy to make a poster or have the gumption to put it up. Support groups for the lackadaisical are non-existent. And if these groups did exist, nobody would ever attend the meetings. Instead, 10 different people would leave the same message on the leader's voicemail: "Hey, something came up. I can't make it tonight. Don't try to call me. I am going to bed early."

I know there are a lot of debilitating diseases, like Fibromyalgia and Chronic Fatigue Syndrome, where a person has a health affliction that makes them constantly tired and prevents them from living a full life. I am not talking about anything as serious as that. I am talking about being a sloth of a human being. Sometimes, I am honest with myself and can admit that I am not going to accomplish bupkis, but sometimes I can truly get tricked into squandering time. In the 21st century, there are a lot of false productivity prophets. There is so much technology—like email, social media, and online chat—that makes you feel that you are doing something productive. It may start out as being worthwhile: "Let me just check on that email," or "I heard that there is a new room doing comedy; let me Google that," or "I need to send out my list of available dates to the comedy bookers." The next thing you know, five hours have passed. You sent that one email, looked at someone's vacation pictures on Instagram, checked your Twitter account eight different times, and got into an instant messaging conversation with someone from your past to whom you were never that close prior to reuniting with them on Facebook. For me, the messaging conversation goes something like this:

"Hey Robin, I hear you're a comedian now."

"Yeah, it's pretty sweet. Making people laugh is awesome. It's my gift to the world."

"I would really like to catch your act sometime!"

"You can always check out my schedule on my website, try to come see me before I totally blow up…LOL!"

In reality, I haven't written a new joke in weeks and have been recycling my best 15 minutes for months. I have notebooks full of funny premises from stuff I have jotted down, but who has time to flesh it out? I have kids, chores, a part-time job, Candy Crush, new episodes of my favorite television programs and, most importantly, writing jokes sometimes feels like real work.

Being lazy is seductive. Nothing feels as good as doing nothing. It seems that any time I go to write, be it jokes for my act, a comedy sketch or even this book, I suddenly become insanely tired. I am not talking sleepy or groggy, but full-blown, "I think this might be my body trying to fight off the flu" tired. I always justify it, too. I think, "I will just power nap or try to meditate." After at least an hour of sleeping, I will wake up and find myself hungry. Not just a little hungry or peckish, but starving. By the time I sleep and then eat, I can convince myself that I need to do just a little bit of housework as well. If I spend my whole day writing, I rationalize to myself, the house will be in disarray, can't have that... Of course, I have done no real writing in the meantime. The only silver lining is that my house actually gets cleaned up a little when I need to write. When I set out to clean the house, I usually end up watching television, so in a way my laziness can fool itself.

I try finding inspiration to control my laziness. Ironically, people post inspirational messages all over Facebook. I read them in my newsfeed, scrolling and scrolling as the hours of my life tick by and I read more and more inspirational quotes. I will read a compelling quote by Eleanor Roosevelt, Benjamin Franklin, or some other dead successful person. "Wow," I think, "that saying really spoke to me. Maybe I will repost it." Then I sit by the computer and see how many people "like" my repost.

Sometimes I try to set a timer. I tell myself that I will write until that timer goes off. It seldom works. I just forget about it or ignore my own rule. The alarm rings, and I find myself Googling something random or looking at social media again and being disappointed that my inspirational quote only got six "likes." I often wonder if maybe a shock collar could be the answer to my lack of focus. If I start to drift away from my goal, I could get buzzed. Who wouldn't want to pursue their dreams using self-punishment and electrodes as an incentive?

In my twenties, I gave myself plenty of leeway. I figured that I was young and had ample time to accomplish my goals. I kept hearing about sowing wild oats and doing what you want in your early adulthood. I guess I thought napping on the couch after a night of drinking was my proverbial "sowing of the oats."

Then time passes in a blink of an eye. It is such a cliché, but it really happens just like that. You live life long enough, and you realize that you're getting older. It's not just a perceived old, like when you turn 25 or 30. Once you are in your forties, the next big mile marker is 50. That is 50 years of being alive, a half of a century, and no matter how you justify it or hear, "Fifty is the new _____," when you have reached that age, you are not a kid anymore. You realize that all the stuff you wanted to do must get done now, or it never will. Time goes by regardless. It doesn't wait for you to have a creative epiphany or be "in the zone."

In the past few years, watching the late-night talk show "Chelsea Lately" on the E! network has inspired me to write more. The show stars Chelsea Handler, who is one of my favorite comedians. I love her moxie. The fact that she isn't especially nice to her guests is awesome. She never does the fake Hollywood interview BS. She will visibly show her irritation with a celebrity, especially if it is a male celebrity. It is so much fun to watch. What I respect and admire most about Chelsea Handler, though, is her writing. She is honest and poignant. She is the same person on paper as she is in person, and to me, that is remarkable. She has had four books on The New York Times Best Seller List and has her own publishing imprint.

On her talk show, Chelsea often discusses how much she hated writing her books. This really influenced me to get off my butt and write, even more so than the fancy smart Facebook quotes ever could. I always imagine professional writers finding satisfaction as they write. I picture authors smiling while typing, smoking pipes and wearing patches on the sleeves of their blazers--which would be weird for women authors, but the mind's eye sees what the mind's eye sees. But I don't think that is always the case. I think a lot of published authors find writing to be horribly tedious, but like runners, they push through the pain to finally reach their goal.

The smartest thing I have done in writing this book was telling my children about my goal to write and publish a book. My kids have not caught on to the fact that I am more of a dreamer than I am a doer. They have actually seen me do stuff. They have seen me write jokes and rehearse my act. They have seen me on stage plenty of times, and they know when I leave the house that I am performing comedy. I have occasionally been able to take them with me on out-of-town gigs. Some of our Florida adventures have enabled us to go to Legoland and the Kennedy Space Center during the day since my gigs are always in the evening. We once took 10 days and went on a "tour" around the Midwest. I recruited Grandma (my Mom) for that undertaking. The four of us traveled to Missouri, Kansas, and Iowa. Our journey gave us such experiences as the kids watching dog races at a casino while eating giant ice cream cones, me begging a hotel clerk to give us a room that didn't reek of cigarettes, and a visit to a four-story water slide that my kids got to go down a zillion times. A few years later, my son was asked to write an essay about a time he will never forget. He wrote about the tour.

My logic in telling my kids that I want to publish a book is basically putting all their trust and credibility on this monumental task that I barely have the confidence in myself to complete. It is like playing blackjack and betting the deed to your house. Time will tell if these words will someday be read by others, or if someday, someone will stumble upon a dusty old Toshiba laptop, fire it up, and read all these many words. I can almost hear their reaction now... "Meh."

Chapter Seven
Not Comedy

Some of my weirdest memories in comedy have nothing to do with the actual show, my material, or my performance on stage. Sometimes you find yourself in a particular location, event, or venue that you would never have been in under any other circumstance. I have had some of the craziest things happen to me just because I was present at a particular moment in the name of comedy. Let me share a few.

Following Hitler: I once did comedy as an intermission for a fancy-schmancy film festival that was held at a Museum of Fine Arts in an upscale area of Fort Myers, Florida. What was supposed to happen was that a film would be shown, and the festival participants would discuss it. I was to follow this up with my act to cleanse the audience's cranial palates, and then they would show the next film. My purpose was to add a light-hearted element as a break in the evening's agenda.

What actually happened was that the first film presented was about a concentration camp during World War II. The plot revolved around a very old Jewish surgeon who was a prisoner in the camp. The head of the camp's son became deathly ill, and the Jewish doctor was called upon to perform surgery on the boy in exchange for his own freedom. The old doctor saved the young

German's life, but refused to be set free since all the other Jewish POWs were still imprisoned. (Who wouldn't be in the mood for comedy after watching that?) Then, after that gut-wrenchingly sad movie—shot in black and white for a greater emotional impact—members of the audience began to argue about the film like only rich, pretentious, artistic-type people could.

"I am really tired of World War II pictures being made. Yes, it was tragic, but it was also 60 years ago. Where are the modern stories that are just as horrific, like Kosovo or Rwanda? Where is that movie of oppression? These World War II movies just keep getting rehashed," interjected one concerned white movie-goer. (Side note: everyone was white.)

The room went abuzz from that comment. Everyone wanted to get their licks into this person for expressing that opinion. Hands waved in the air. My stomach fell to my knees. "Great segue into comedy—Nazis and a passive-aggressive snark fest," I thought to myself. I could feel yet another embarrassing comedy failure coming on.

Another person stood up and said, "My Grandfather was a World War II veteran, and I don't think there can be enough of these types of films. Never forget!" The room exploded in applause. More hands went in the air. So many people wanted to comment, everyone was fired up, and I started to feel that first pang of diarrhea.

After what seemed like an eternity of pissed-off smart people talk, it was finally time for me to do my set. In all the commotion of the heated debate, no one had ever turned the projector off—so I went on stage with the movie screen still down and the title menu showing. The title menu had an image of Hitler in the top corner of the screen, scowling and staring down at me while I performed my silly material about shopping at Aldi Discount Grocery Store and the wacky shit my kids say. Thanks FDR and Churchill for freeing the world so people like me can go on to tell dumb jokes in the name of art.

I am not Debbie: Open mics come and go. The best ones, like the best comedy shows, are at actual comedy clubs, but from time to time a bar will try an open mic comedy night. One particular evening, I decided to check out a new open mic that a friend of mine was trying to start. It was like so many open mics I have gone to…horrible. The other bar patrons did not know it was anything more than a regular Tuesday night at this establishment. The stage was set up away from the bar. The bar was surrounded by televisions—televisions that were still on and broadcasting a baseball playoff game. No one was sitting in the designated chairs that had been set up for the comedy open mic. Everyone was at the bar.

Most comics just went on stage and soldiered through their sets. At least the other comics in the room were paying attention, but the chatter at the bar was growing louder and louder. I was honestly thinking of either leaving or just doing what everyone else was doing and half-assing it from the stage. But as my luck would have it, the comic who went on before me took the wireless mic up to the bar and did his set from there. It got mixed results since most people really wanted to watch the game, but a few people paid attention to him. It also set the precedent that the rest of the comedy show was to be conducted at that spot rather than on the stage. I was next, and I bombed, to say the least. The last guy at least had pot jokes to fall back on. I had a few drinking jokes that they laughed at, but then I ate it for the rest of my set.

I did not let bombing there get me down, not like I would have had it been earlier in my career, especially under these circumstances. I just chalked it off as a bad night at a venue that was not at all conducive to comedy. I wanted go home, snuggle up with my kids, and let this evening become a distant memory. I said my goodbyes and starting walking to my car. In the parking lot I heard, "Debbie! Debbie!" Of course, I didn't look up since my name is Robin. Then I felt a hand on my elbow. I turned around. There stood a short, hefty older lady with a cane.

She looked a little startled at first. "Oh, I am sorry," she said in a Southern drawl. "I thought you was Debbie and you and me was about to have words."

"Excuse me?" I asked. Now, I grew up in a small town. I speak fluent redneck and have had my share of scrapes outside of a bar. This old woman was drunk and wanted to stir up some shit. I wasn't scared of her; I just was not in the mood for a parking lot smack-down with a senior citizen. I had made an ass of myself trying to perform comedy to a bar full of people who wanted to watch baseball. I was tired and was so not interested in her drama with Debbie.

Like most drunks, she kept repeating herself. "You are lucky that you ain't Debbie, cause you and me was about to have words," she said, over and over again.

"Nope, I am not Debbie. I am just leaving," I told her.

"Debbie is the whore that used to be married to my son," she replied, answering a question I had never asked or even cared to ask.

"We'll Ma'am, I am sorry, but I am not her," I repeated. Then I turned to walk back to my car.

"If you was her, you and me was going to have words...!" she said yet again. "My son is the bartender here and that bitch fucked him over. You and me was about to have words."

"Well, Debbie sounds awful. I am a comedian, not a whore, and I was just here for a comedy open mic. I am leaving now," I explained, quickly losing my patience with this exchange.

Luckily, a friend of mine, another comedian, walked up on our conversation. My friend was there to check out the open mic as well. That distracted the old lady. After telling my friend that she thought I was Debbie and how lucky I was not to be Debbie, the tubby old woman hobbled away on her cane, hell-bent on saving her son's honor.

Cowboy Up: One of the two big comedy clubs in Tampa is located in an area of town called Ybor City. Ybor City is similar to the French Quarter in New Orleans, Westport in Kansas City, and Beal St. in Memphis. It is a historical area of the city that has shops, bars, and restaurants, but it is predominately known as the party area of town. There is an open mic night every Wednesday at the comedy club in Ybor City. The open mic is not located in the showroom where the main stage is. Instead, it is held in the bar area of the club on a stage in the corner of the room. It starts at 10 PM after the Wednesday regular show is finished, and it attracts a really tough crowd. It is very loud, and no one really listens to you while you are doing your set. The customers who have been to the main show and stay after it has ended are pretty much tired of comedy at that point, and they are drunk. The few people who come just for the open mic are also drunk. The comics are often drunk, or at least buzzed, as well. (You almost have to be to perform on that stage.) I have had a few good sets, but it is rare; performing there is usually like screaming into the wind.

There used to be a small bar down the street from the comedy club. It was called the Lower Red, and it had fantastic drink specials, like a small glass of cheap beer and a shot of rot-gut whiskey for $2. As a general rule, I am not a shot drinker of any kind, but this got to be a social habit for the comedians who performed at the Wednesday open mic night. Just one, sometimes two rounds, would chill you just enough to handle the horror of that stage.

Most bars have crazy names, so I did not really question this one. It was a family owned bar. Two dark-haired, very pretty sisters were the bartenders. They were always nice and as per usual with living in Tampa, I just assumed they were Hispanic. One of the sisters remembered that my hands shake and would always put my whiskey in a tumbler rather than a shot glass so I would not spill it.

One evening, I was meeting another comedian there—a good friend whom I affectionately call "M'lady." She was the person who had originally started the tradition of drinking at the Lower Red on Wednesdays. I had come in and begun chatting with my friend when one of the sister bartenders asked us if we were ready to order. I said, "I am ready to cowboy-up and have a beer and a shot. How about you, M'lady?"

M'lady agreed and smiled politely, but when the bartender left, she began scolding me. "What the fuck is wrong with you?" she yelled. "Why are you saying that shit to her?"

"What did I say?" I asked, genuinely puzzled.

"Why are you being a dick with all that cowboy shit? You know they are Native Americans," M'lady continued, her Queens, N.Y. accent thickening with every curse word.

"No, I didn't know," I said earnestly. "I thought they were Hispanic."

"You're racist. Why would Hispanic people name their bar Lower Red, you asshole?" she asked.

"Why would Native Americans name their own bar, Lower Red? That is racist, not me," I retorted.

We saw the bartender coming back and stopped our conversation. Soon after that, the bar went out of business. I never thought the term "cowboy-up" was particularly offensive, and may have still used that term even with the knowledge of the bartender ladies' heritage. I still remember that night, and M'lady still thinks I am an asshole.

The Zombie Apocalypse- On Cinco De Mayo of last year, I had another gig in Fort Myers. (It is donning on me now that wacky stuff seems to happen there.) This gig was at a hotel in their downtown area. I carpooled with my friend Annisa, who is also a comedian, and her boyfriend, John. We left Tampa early to give ourselves enough time to get our bearings and grab something to eat. It was a Saturday, and the traffic in Ft. Myers was insane. As we were looking for a parking spot, we saw two people dressed up like it was Halloween. They had white makeup on their faces and fake blood around their mouths. I didn't think much of it, as crazy people are a common sighting in Florida.

After circling the downtown area for twenty minutes, John dropped Annisa and me off at a pizza parlor in walking distance of the hotel where the gig was to be held and parked in a parking garage that was blocks away. While we were in the pizza parlor waiting for John, we saw another person with their face painted white. Then we continued to see more and more people made up to look like the un-dead.

Annisa, who is Puerto Rican and Salvadoran, thought the people were dressing as La Catrina, a Mexican symbol for death. It is a tradition to dress as her for the Day of the Dead. Annisa could not figure out why they were decked out like that on Cinco De Mayo rather than on All Saints Day.

When John returned from parking the car, we had dinner and then decided to make our way to the hotel. The pizza place's front entrance was on the street, but it had a back entrance that was connected to an outdoor mall area that had other shops and restaurants. A stage was being set up in the mall area, and it looked like there was going to be an outdoor concert. We left through the rear entrance so we could check things out—and because it was a shortcut to the hotel.

As we were walking, someone asked us if we had bought our wrist band yet. We had no idea what he was talking about. Then he asked, "Aren't you here for the festival?"

We told him that we were just cutting through to get to our gig at the nearby hotel. This, of course, led to us to explain that we were comedians from out of town. He said, "Well if you get out early, come back by here. Tonight is Zombie Con. It is the biggest zombie festival in the U.S."

Once the man told us about Zombie Con, we finally understood why all the people in the mall looked like death, literally. We continued to speak with the man as the place got more crowded with people dressed up as zombies. That was the first I had heard of any type of zombie convention.

Finally, we left the man and found our hotel. It was a really nice hotel, and the room/bar where we were to do our comedy show was really cool. The décor was very artsy and trendy. There were black leather couches, and the stage was lit with an assortment of colored lights. It would have been a great place to have a drink and listen to a jazz combo. The room was not particularly conducive to comedy, though. The stage was in the corner, and only a few couches and high-top tables were directly in front of the stage. The bar was on the right side of the stage, and there was an automatic door to the left. We knew right away that if the doors opened and people walked in, they would walk right in front of the stage. We were right; it happened a lot that night. The later the hour, the more often the doors opened to unsuspecting zombies who strolled past us while we tried to perform. Some stayed, and most walked on by, but that was the first time I could say the crowd was really dead and mean it.

Mrs. (Non-Disclosure) Claus(e): I am kind of a cheap person. I rarely go to malls. I find them to be horribly over-priced. I love discount stores, thrift shops, or any place I can find a bargain. One Christmas season, while spending a Saturday at a local flea market, I noticed a sign for a Santa. After rounding the corner, I saw him in all his glory, a flea market Kris Kringle. He was just as good as any mall Santa. He had a giant chair with a colorful background. He was surrounded by children and was peddling pictures to their parents. The only difference was, his photos were only $5, and his beard was real.

I was sold. The flea market became the official Christmas Santa Stop for my children from that day forward. I have years of pictures adorning my mantle at Christmas time with the kids and Flea Market Santa. You can see the changes in my kids' growth through the years. In the first few photos, they are both chubby and smiling. In the later ones, their faces have thinned out. There came to a point one year that my son no longer wanted to be a part of the Santa photo. He was not ready to say with 100% certainty that there was no Santa, and he liked the yearly gifts, but he did not want to go as far as to get his picture taken with Jolly Old St. Nick anymore. He had his friends over to the house on a regular basis, and he had his "rep" to protect.

A couple of Christmases ago, I took only my daughter to see Flea Market Santa. The nice part about this Santa is there aren't any crazy lines; you usually just have to wait for a few people ahead of you. When we got there, a little boy was getting his photo taken with Santa, and then it would be my daughter's turn next. We waited patiently for the boy. The picture-taking itself didn't take long, but the mother was not happy, so she wanted the photo to be redone. Then, she was not sure how many pictures she wanted. She was on her cell phone consulting with someone, and when she finally made up her mind, the printer jammed. In the meantime, my daughter was quietly waiting.

This particular year, Santa wasn't alone in his chair; he was accompanied by his lovely wife, Mrs. Claus.

While we were waiting for the printer to be fixed, Santa waved my daughter over and asked her what she wanted for Christmas (which is always a second thought these days in any Santa situation, it is usually the exchange of picture money that takes precedent). As Katie and Santa were chatting, I was recognized by Mrs. Santa. "Hey aren't you that comedian?" she asked.

Normally those words are music to my ears and harmonious to my fragile ego. Under any other circumstance, I would have been more than happy to talk about my favorite subject, me. But this was Katie's moment. It was the day she had been waiting for all season, to tell a magical man what material goods that she wanted most as a gift. I wasn't sure how to handle it. "Yes," I replied, trying to give her the polite, "Please stop talking; my kid can hear you" plea with my eyes. It did not work.

"I am a friend of Sandy Peterson, and we all came and saw you and the Hilarious Hustlas when you played at the Millwood Cantina," she said, ignoring her costume and the façade that it represented. Again, I tried pleading with my eyes, this time whispering, "That was a fun night. I am here with my little girl; she really wanted to get her picture with Santa." I looked over and Katie was chatting away with Flea Market Father Time. I prayed that she had not heard any of this conversation.

In the meantime, the previous customer was still dealing with her order and the jammed printer. Mrs. Claus just kept on talking. "Why don't you get in the picture with us?" she asked.

"Oh that's okay. This is for Katie, right, honey?" I said to my daughter, who at that point had an uncomfortable expression on her face. It looked like she had run out of things to talk to Santa about.

"I don't mind, Mommy," my daughter said in all her sweetness.

"Here, just scoot next to Santa," Mrs. Claus told Katie, and then instructed me to sit between the two of them.

The bench they were sitting on was made for the Christmas couple and a child or two, not three grown adults and one little girl. I tried sitting between Katie and Mrs. Claus. "It is a tight fit. I will just stand to the side," I said, trying desperately to get out of this situation.

"Nonsense," Mrs. Claus said. "You can sit on my lap." She pulled me down onto her, and there I was, half on her lap, half trying to balance myself with my arm next to my daughter. Mrs. Claus kept talking about comedy the whole time.

"Where will you guys be playing next? We had so much fun that night," she babbled. I sat there praying that the "helper elves" would finally be finished with their previous customer. At last, it was our turn to get the picture taken. We all had big smiles, but mine was less of a smile and more a grimace from the tops of my thighs that were burning from me not wanting to put all my weight on Mrs. Claus.

When we were finally done taking and then buying the photo, Katie and I were walking through the flea market to leave. I tried to divert Katie's attention. I had no idea how I was going to handle the inevitable questions.

"You want to eat something fried?" I asked her. Katie did not take the bait.

"Mommy you're famous!" she said, looking up at me adoringly. "Santa's wife knew who you were!"

I scrambled to come up with an answer. "I think in the off season, they may sneak away from the North Pole, you know, to go out, grab a bite to eat with their friends and maybe see a show," I said. "I guess you never know who is in the audience on any given night."

Katie left it at that. Maybe at 7, she didn't want to admit that she had figured it all out. She may have been hedging her bets like her brother, and did not want to rock the boat so close to Christmas morning. Or maybe she had bought it…hook, line, and sinker. Maybe she thought I was to the North Pole what David Hasselhoff was to Germany. Either way, we both walked out of the giant swap meet with a photo in our hand and a memory of the day Mommy met her biggest fan, Mrs. Santa Claus.

MY CHARACTERS

Chapter Eight
If Cats Could Speak

I am Calvin A. Tabby. I am a cat. Yes, I realize that my name is also an anagram for CAT. I am a cat, for God's sake. We are the masters of word play, irony, and satire. You humans just see us as string-playing, finicky little beings that you feed kibble to. Oh, you clueless people, with your "kitty condos" and your gritty sand boxes that you put in your climate-controlled, horribly decorated homes for us to shit in. How very generous of you. Your species is so smug and superior. You just assume that we are here for your amusement. We "kitties," with our furry coats and agile bodies, are so cute--that is, we were, before the impending revolution. The day of reckoning is soon coming to the flesh-exposed, two-legged, walking upright beasts you all are.

Until then, I am formally petitioning on behalf of all cats to stop the defamation of felines on the Internet. I am proposing the People Unnecessarily Smearing a Species Act. (Yes, I realize that it is an anagram for PUSS. I am a cat, for God's sake.) This World Wide Web, as it is called, is an omnipresent technology that you humans built to communicate and educate, yet it is being used to smear the cat community. Rather than transcending our current state of being with this high-tech tool, you humans use it exploit the idiosyncrasies of felines. You find our ways so amusing. You humans think our behavior is adorable, rather than the calculated actions of beings functioning at a level higher than any of you human could possibly achieve. We master so much, but are understood little.

There are countless online memes and pictures and videos depicting us as brainless scamps looking for mischief. The worst offender of all is a website that features nothing but cats' faces being smooshed through a piece of bread. It doesn't even make sense. A cat and a piece of white bread have nothing in common. Again, this endless degradation is all for the amusement of you Neanderthals who hail yourselves as the superior beings. The horror of it all is mind-boggling.

Even when you humans aren't using actual pictures of us, you are still desecrating our likeness. Years ago, an animated cartoon called "Nyan Cat" surfaced. It was a cheap graphic of a Pop Tart with a cat's head flying through the air shooting rainbows out of its backside and all set to a repetitive horrible digital tune. This video has gotten millions of hits. Can you guess how many times it was viewed by an actual cat? The answer would be "none."

Cats are not the time-wasters that you humans are. We don't squander our nine lives on video games and social media. We are more worried about science, physics, and studying the building blocks of the universe. Most feline quantum discoveries have surpassed anything that is currently being studied in your human world. That is why we are always sleeping in small boxes. It is critical to figuring out the space-time continuum, while embodying as little space as possible. The concept itself couldn't possibly be understood by your homo sapien brain. To you, it is just another adorable kitty antic, so you click pictures and post them online anytime we put ourselves inside of a box or a paper bag.

Years ago, a scientist, a young Steven Hawking, got a little too close to understanding these techniques. We made sure his communication was limited from then on. Who controls the voice box of the computer that Hawking speaks through? Oh, I wonder. So many times he has actually said, "Help, I am being enslaved by cats." Instead, the digital voice comes on and states one of our brilliant observations about the cosmos.

Unfortunately, this anti-feline crusade has been going on since even before the Internet was invented. Although technology merely exacerbates the defamation, it has been happening for decades. In the 1970's, there were equally offensive posters that had become all the rage. One particularly popular poster depicted a kitten barely hanging onto a tree branch with the "hilarious" caption, "Hang in there, Baby." That adorable scamp photographed was none other than Rutherford "Boots" Meriman, one of our most famous chemists, who single - handedly discovered compound elements that you humans are still decades away from comprehending. To us, he was a star, but to you humans, he was a cubicle accessory to help those in mind-numbing, dead-end jobs to be inspired to live another day.

Humiliated and disheartened, Boots spent his final days in an abandoned shed as a feral, with a two-gram-a-day catnip habit. It finally became too much for him to bear, so late in the night, he ate a poinsettia leaf and left the following message in the sand: "I could hang on no longer."

The most recent feline to be shot to your human fame is the poor creature deemed "Grumpy Cat." Her notoriety became my last straw. An animal that had her mouth inverted is all of a sudden the quintessential pessimist. Newsflash to you all-important beings with fur only on your heads: Not everyone who frowns is automatically thinking negative thoughts. "Grumpy Cat," or "Tartar Sauce" as she was deemed by her horrid owners, is a poet, musician, and philosopher. She can play a concerto in C minor that can bring even a longshoreman to tears. To see the finest of our artists being played up as a hero of cynicism is more than I can handle. I hope that she can deal with all the fame that comes her way. Despite the turned-down mouth, her natural optimism and grace should carry her through such trying times.

Every night, I pray for opposable thumbs so that I may log on to those annoying glowing computers. I would then be the one making memes and taking photos of you men and women chasing a ball of string, or standing next to a broken flower bed. I would put the same ridiculous captions on you humans' pictures, like: "Ize likes u," "Nom Nom Nom," or "Me don't know what happened," the same way you do to us. As if that is what we would say if we could speak the primitive language of the humans. We mostly assuredly would not misspell any words.

Even the music industry has joined in on the defamation of felines. The skinny girl who sticks her tongue out on a regular basis, the human called Myley Cyrus, went on an awards show and sang her latest song while a picture of a cat lip-syncing the lyrics was playing on a giant screen behind her. Again, a small kitten would never agree to be a part of something as droll as pop music. The music that only we can create is usually more in line with Tchaikovsky than with the daughter of a has-been, mullet-haired country singer. It is all we can do not to unleash our claws and rip out the voice boxes of the entire music industry after we see these types of spectacles.

You humans pollute the world and wonder why it is dirty .You use all your water for grooming and cleansing yourselves and then wonder why you ran out of water. You humans have cabinets full of beauty and hygiene supplies, but all the while, cats have glossy, glistening coats and clean bodies with our mere saliva. Cats only use water modestly for drinking. If cats ruled the planet, we would never waste natural resources that are currently being squandered for the sake of vanity. We are much too self-sufficient. You humans hurt your giant bulbous heads every day wondering about the many mysteries of the universe: crop circles, Stonehenge, pyramids. Oh, how mysterious, indeed…meow.

Chapter Nine
Soccer Mom Sienna

I just drove home from dropping off the kids at school. I got to show off my personalized license plates—SIECEDES. It stands for Sienna (Me) and my Mercedes (my new car). I adore that car. I do not let the kids eat, drink, or roll down the windows in it. I just love the smell of the new leather seats.

It was my day to chauffer the carpool. I usually have my Zumba/Spin/Cardio Kick Boxing class in the mornings, but on my driving days I have to compensate for my absence by not eating any carbs. We all have to make sacrifices for our children. Tomorrow, when it's Brianna's day to drive the carpool, I will work out double to make up for it by wearing my 15-pound leg shackles on the elliptical machine. Being a Mom in the twenty-first century requires you to remain in peak physical condition and to have properly highlighted hair.

Today stands to be stressful as it is. First, I have the upholstery cleaners coming over to steam the ottoman for the third time this month. My husband, Roland, fought me about getting a white sofa since we have school-aged children. I told him, kids or no kids, we need to have nice furniture. What does he expect? Does he want us to live with plastic on our couch? We aren't animals or Italians. He asked me, "Sienna, just who are we trying to impress?" He is so naïve. Who aren't we trying to impress? It is called being a grown-up. He just sighs and heads to his home office, which is our extra bedroom that used to be the guest room.

When we first moved into the East Catch neighborhood, everyone was getting the five-bedroom houses. They all have the same floor plan as well. Most of us in the neighborhood had our houses painted a modest, low-key taupe, but we have some rabble-rousers down the street who chose sandstone. I wrote them a properly worded, anonymous letter about how they are bringing down the property value. They are the same neighbors who tried to put the blow-up Frosty the Snowman next to the giant blow-up nativity scene on their front lawn during Christmas. Can you imagine? I personally called for an emergency civic association meeting to put the kibosh on that nonsense. Holidays are about showing class and low-key decorum—like my Christmas tree that is adorned only with ornaments from Tiffany & Co. The neighbors cannot see them from the front yard, but they are featured prominently in the holiday edition of my monthly newsletter.

When we first bought the house, Roland kept blathering on about us overextending ourselves, but I told him that the extra rooms would come in handy someday. I was so right, as usual. When the rest of the ladies on the block started having babies, I gave Roland more "sexy" bedroom privileges than ever. He was so happy…then. Now, 12 years later, we have our precious angels, Evan and Hannah. They each have their own room, and Roland has his home office. I originally thought about making it my in-home gym, but if I did not show up for my morning exercise classes, who would know what kind of dedication I have to my well being? Also, who would take attendance and report the absences on our exclusive, neighborhood-only Facebook Group Page? Then again, my size 2 yoga pants don't wear themselves, now do they?

Roland has taken on more responsibility at work, which keeps him in that office for hours on end. Some days, we do not even see him. I hate to admit it, but it is for the best. His parenting style is very authoritarian. It is nothing at all like the parenting style that is discussed in the books that I, along with the rest of gals in the neighborhood, have read. Roland learned to be a father from his father, who, by the way, drove a used car until the day he died. Every vehicle that man ever owned had an upholstered interior. It is sad when you think about it, never knowing the smell of new leather seats. Choosing leather seats is like a giving a gift to your nose that reminds you that you are a little better than the other drivers on the road.

Roland is very, "I make the rules, I pay the bills, and you listen to me" with the kids. I am constantly quoting the new styles of parenting to him. My favorite book is "Rejoice in Your Children, Rejoice in Your Life." I tell Hannah and Evan each day what a special gift they are to Mommy, to the neighborhood, and to the universe. Contrary to Roland's constant grumbling, I have children with self esteem out the roof. Hannah has already told me that she plans on affording a lifestyle where she never has to lower herself to do manual labor. She has never washed a dish in her life and says she never plans to. She is goal-setting at ten years old, and I could not be prouder. Evan is constantly telling his teachers how much smarter he is than the other students. I cannot tell you how many times I have been hauled into a parent/teacher conference and his instructor had the audacity to insinuate that Evan is pompous. I feel bad that these so-called "educators" have not taken the time to educate themselves like I have about rearing confident children. On a side note, every one of the teachers at his school also drives a used car (snicker).

Also today, I have to help organize the school's fundraiser. It is a private school, which means they need more funding than the public schools to keep up with a certain standard that the school has set. The public schools in the area only have one fundraiser per year. They usually sell chocolate bars, cookie dough, or something pedestrian. Not this school. The PTSCFBF (The Parent Teacher Student Committee For a Better Future) decided to do a monthly fundraiser. We have had some really classy ones too: organic breads, handmade artisan jewelry and Tiffany & Co. ornaments. Many of our relatives have starting avoiding us like the plague, especially the ones on Roland's side of the family. It infuriates me, since I bought five chocolate bars from his nephew last Thanksgiving. I did not eat them, of course. They were milk chocolate rather than dark chocolate, and any chocolate bar that has less than 85% cocoa in it, I give to the neighborhood kids for trick-or-treat. I also bought one of those coupon books from Roland's paunchy niece. It was $25 for something that I will never use, like I would be caught using a coupon anyway. Besides, they don't accept coupons at the Organic Grocery Store in our neighborhoods, where we all shop. (I don't want to rock the boat with the school, so I usually buy enough of Hannah and Evan's monthly fundraiser items as to not have any suspicious eyes raised at us. We can afford it. Roland has been working extra hours.)

The fundraiser we are working on now is a school carnival—not a real one, of course, but a simulated one. We would not want to expose the children who attend East Catch Preparatory of Higher Learning to carnie-folk. This would be more of a home-spun carnival. The big dust-up from the last meeting was whether to allow the public to attend our fundraiser. Always the diplomat that I am, I listened to both sides before forming the opinion that I had already established. On the one hand, it would give us a chance to collect money from people besides the ones who always contribute to the school. But then how would inviting in the outside world into our school make the outsiders feel? Children who attend local schools would be allowed in our hallowed halls for one night only. They would see how much they are missing out on at their publicly funded institutions. How depressing that would be for them.

Think of it. They would see our drinking fountains, each one with a plaque that commemorates the generous people who donated money for it. (Now that was a fundraiser! We called it Fondues for Fountains. We had a giant fondue party, we used only imported cheeses, and all the proceeds went to the fountains and the cheese.) There are three plaques commemorating our family for donating water fountains. One is for Hannah, one is for Evan, and the other has only my name on it. I asked Roland if he wanted it to have his name on it too. He was so mad that I had donated $500 per fountain that he did not speak to me for a week. I took that act of not being a team player as a "no," so a plaque with just my name, Sienna Hutchison, proudly hangs above the 2nd floor hallway fountain next to the girls' bathroom. They wanted to hang it near the janitor's closet, but I pulled a few strings and got a spot a little more befitting of someone who selflessly volunteers like I do.

The carnival will be in three weeks. We finally came to the decision to make it an invitation-only event. Roland asked me once, "Why do you mess with all these extra expenses? It is the same people giving money but for different fundraisers; the school should just be up front and charge us an extra $5K a year rather than force us to deal with this bullshit." Poor Roland, I often think. Coming from his humble background, he does not understand the importance of a social structure and a sense of community. Besides, the Volunteer of the Year Award is coming up and I cannot lose to Gwen Ledbetter, not again.

Gwen is the bane of my existence. She thinks she is so superior to me with her nouveau riche Cadillac Escalade and her sandstone house. She would not know subtlety and good taste if it bit her right in her Bedazzled track suit. I do not like to gossip, but she only attends the exercise classes twice a week, and when she does she constantly announces her resting and exercising heart rate. It is so petty. It shows what type of person she really is. Like anyone cares, plus my resting heart rate is always much lower than hers.

Gwen thought we should have a cotton candy machine and popcorn at the carnival. Oh, please...Why don't we just have McDonalds cater it? Why don't we all move into double-wide trailers and have a hoe-down instead of a carnival? Gwen is infuriating.

When I got to the meeting, Gwen had arrived early. She was showing off her new iPhone cover. Like most of Gwen's possessions, it is encrusted with rubies and rhinestones. She had also made a scale model of the carnival out of papier mache. It is like she has nothing better to do with her time. It was in that moment that I was thankful that I had taken three full days to put together my PowerPoint slide show, complete with an estimated budget of what the carnival that I want will cost versus how much is earned. I bet Gwen didn't crunch the numbers like I did. It is all about presentation and looks with her. She really doesn't understand substance.

It ended up being a very long meeting. I could tell that the other people on the committee were becoming impatient. They kept trying to interrupt me during my Power Point presentation by pointing to their watches. Gwen had the nerve to give me the "wrap it up" signal by twirling her index finger in the air. It was all I could do to keep my composure.

"I guess if deciding on the details of a simulated carnival to help our privileged students get updated versions of equipment that the school already has, seems like a waste of time, then I can't help you," I told them sternly. I hate to be so heavy-handed, but sometimes you have to tell people the truth. I continued, "If lavishing our young children with material items isn't a true indicator of how we are doing collectively as parents, then I guess I don't know what being a good parent is."

They all looked uncomfortable, and I knew what they were thinking. "Of course Sienna is a good parent. She outlines the reasons every month in her newsletter." As I continued with my proposed ideas, I knew I was going to win and have the carnival the way I wanted it. I could see it in their eyes; it was that look of defeat, of being beaten by a superior opponent. I see it every day in Roland's eyes, too. I like to think that is the universe's way of telling me that I am on the right track.

I walked out of that meeting the victor. I took pride in knowing that I had made a difference. I got to preserve the reputation of our school for having the latest, most state-of-the-art technology of all of the private schools in the tri-county region. I am like a soldier, really. Every month is a new battle. This month it was a contrived carnival. Next month it may be a silent auction or raffle for a day spa. I will continue to fight the good fight until I win the war—the war on good taste, the war on Gwen Ledbetter, and the war on my relevance to the world.

Chapter Ten
Cathy Gainer, Corporate Trainer

Hi Gang, my name is Cathy Gainer. I am a corporate trainer, personal life coach, spiritual crossing guard, and motivational mentor for hire. I have had a lot of jobs, most of which have included two weeks of training. Since I usually get fired from my jobs, I have been through a lot of new-hire classes.

One day I had an epiphany. It was like Oprah's "a-ha moment," but with more syllables. I decided to conduct new-hire training for life. As the old saying goes, "Life doesn't come with an instruction manual." But now it comes with a two-week orientation class. I facilitate a course that lets you become familiar with life's rules, regulations, and attendance policies. My first module is Sexual Harassment Training. It includes an instructional video that I made in my basement with an unsuspecting Terminix Man (lawsuit still pending). It also comes with "The Gainer Guide." It is a simple-to-follow, 72-point plan that outlines most of life's lessons. Some of the topics include:

1. If you fail to win, you win at failing.
2. Do you want success or does success want you?
3. Strive for perfection while perfectly striving.
4. Ask a question or question your asking.
5. If loving me is wrong, I don't wanna be right.

6. Who fermented my cheese?

7. The one-second secretary.

8. The Known Fact (an alternative to The Secret)

9. Misquotes and false statistics for use on social media

10. Why the customer is always write(ing) (complaints)

11. How to be your own passive-aggressive friend.

12. What makes a good catchphrase and what is considered "plagiarizing"?

13. How to curb negative self-talk, unless you like being a complete douche bag.

14. Lean in, pretend you dropped something and then run.

15. Job Creator Mom, Food Stamp Mom

16. Knowledge is a power bottom.

17. How to maintain your integrity while washing your boss's car.

18. Developing leadership skills at home by outsourcing family members.

19. Is it gratitude or just settling?

20. Being assertive…with a baseball bat.

This is just some of the fun that you can expect. Now you may be wondering, what makes my program different than my peers' programs? Well, motivational speakers Tony Robbins, Ken Blanchard, and the estate of Stephen Covey have repeatedly requested that I stop referring to them as peers (lawsuit still pending). These other motivational speakers also have programs that are costly or come with a tedious PBS commercial. My program is a lot easier on the old pocketbook. I do not necessarily need cash. I am a strong believer in the barter system. I once helped a young man turn his life around in exchange for fast food gift certificates and an occasional coupon. That same young man also went on to get accepted into his county's most prestigious community college. Today, he is at his same job with the same salary, but he has a lot more student loans to pay off. With my help, dreams can come true. (Incidentally, if you are thinking about trying my program and you want to use coupons, please be sure they have not expired and that they come from a real restaurant or store. Taco Bell doesn't consider a "One Free Hug "voucher to be legal tender, no matter how many times you reach into the drive-through window).

I also tackle the subjects of love and relationships. Now for full disclosure, I never actually gone on a "date" or even associated with or been touched by another human being in a romantic way, but I am a studier. I have studied many young lovers having a night of romance (lawsuit still pending), and I have watched all 249 episodes of "The Love Boat," so I know of what I speak. Same-sex couples are welcome, too. "The Gainer Guide" does not discriminate when it comes to intimacy. (The hug vouchers apparently are also not considered legal tender with gay or straight couples either, no matter how many times you reach in through their windows.)

Some couples may opt for my weekend getaway package. It includes a three- day, two-night stay at a luxurious KOA campground of your choice. You will be whisked there in my 1969 Gremlin, hitched to my "gently used" pop-up trailer (or my home, as I like to call it). Again, I offer cost-effective rates. I only charge the camping fee (less my KOA discount), and you have to pack enough provisions to share with me. I would prefer chicken salad to tuna salad, but deli-sliced turkey is my sandwich of choice. Any fresh fruit is fine, but try to limit your alcohol intake. On my last getaway package trip, I thought the couple had brought poultry seasoning, so I marinated the meal with a bottle of their Wild Turkey. The next morning, we all woke up to the local animals rummaging through the trailer, which had been moved to a more exotic location—the middle of the busy off-ramp next to the KOA. Since that night, I unfortunately have to charge extra for the incense that I continuously burn to offset the musky "I think it was a cat that peed in here, but it may have been a raccoon" smell that now permeates the trailer.

In addition to the change of scenery that I offer on the getaway, I will conduct marriage/relationship-building courses and games, which include "The Gainer Guide's Exclusive Pair-Bonding Exercises":

1. **Who is a better spouse?:** Couples debate who works harder in the relationship.

2. **I remember when**: An exercise that allows us to bring up past arguments and relive them.

3. **I wonder what _____ is doing now?** This is when the couple each brings up past relationships and tries to figure out whether or not they would have been better off with an ex-lover.

4. **You aren't prettier than _____.** (For the ladies)

5. **You don't listen to me like _____'s husband does.** (For the gentlemen)

6. **Who has the more over-bearing mother?**

7. **My Biggest Regret Roulette:** Each partner spins a wheel and tells their spouse what they sacrificed for their mate.

8. **I Would Rather:** Couples list activities they would rather do instead of spending time with their partner.

9. **Condescending Password**: Participants try to get their partner to guess the answer to one of their proudest accomplishments by giving them condescending clues.

Clue 1: "Boo-hoo, I sacrificed having anything nice for five years."

Clue 2: "I am soooo much smarter than everyone else now."

Clue 3: "I got to go to a ceremony and dress like a judge with a fancy hat in front of people."

Answer: "The time I put myself through graduate school?"

10. **Bad Marriage Bingo**: Each partner is handed a card with 25 squares. Each square has an obnoxious or habit or behavior printed on it. I will call out such behaviors as "Looks at other women while we are on *date night*", "runs up credit card debt without the other person's knowledge" or "hasn't groomed intimate regions since honeymoon." If a behavior is on the card AND the spouse is guilty of it, then they get to cover the square with a bingo dobber. The winner gets the knowledge of being the most at fault in the relationship and an autographed copy of "The Gainer Guide."

Although these courses and games have not technically been implemented during my getaway weekend, they have scored high with a few test groups.

The subjects did not actually know this was part of a couples' counseling program. They were more upset by my intrusive questions and wondered why I had repeatedly entered their tent, bearing hug coupons (lawsuit pending, and my KOA membership is on temporary suspension).

I am also starting a new and exciting weight loss plan called "Gaining to Lose." It uses only blended drinks for your daily calorie intake. This is great for people who squander hours shopping for the freshest fruits and vegetables. Now your food comes to you monthly by mail in a big brown box. Who needs nature when you have UPS? If you follow my strict regimen of drinking only expensive shakes, supplied solely by me, you are guaranteed to shed pounds and inches before your body thinks it starving and causes you to eat ravenously and uncontrollably.

I had been working on a new calorie-counting app for people with a phone. I had gotten very close to achieving great success. It would have let you add all the calories that you ate each day, but subtract all of the exercise that burned the calories off. Unfortunately, my app wasn't able to calculate one's BMI, the value of any calories in any given food, or the amount of calories actually burned while exercising. However, the beauty of this app was that you did not need a smart phone to use it—any phone would do. I was going to call it the Gainer-Calc App. When I pitched it to the major cellular carriers, they told me that my idea for an app was just the calculator that was already installed on every phone, and then they asked to leave the mall kiosk.

As you can see, my life is very productive. My goal is to teach others what I have never been able to learn myself, and each day I am getting closer to not learning even more. If you were to ask me what I have gleaned through the years of being a trainer (no one has asked), I would say that the most important things to do are to stay busy, never give up—and legally change your name every few years to throw off the creditors.

MY REAL LIFE

Chapter Eleven
Save Anna

I grew up in Savannah, Missouri. It is a small rural area that my family moved to when I was five years old. I consider it my hometown, and most of my high school friends still live near there. I associate myself with that town so much that I use a stage name of Savage, the high school's mascot, as homage to that crazy little spot on the map where I spent 15 of my formative years. We were the Savannah Savages, and I wanted to give a wink and a nod to my past as I pursued comedy. I left Savannah in 1990 and lived in Kansas City, Missouri for five years and have now lived in Florida for almost 20 years, but I still identify myself as a Midwesterner.

I once heard that Savannah got its name from the wagon trains making their way across the prairie back in the 1800's. A little girl named Anna fell from one of the wagons. Her frightened mother screamed, "Stop! Save Anna! Save Anna!" The wagon trains came to a screeching halt and rescued the girl, while the pioneers liked the area so much that they settled there and named it "Savannah" for Save Anna. This story is not true, of course. Savannah was founded in 1841 and was originally called Union, but the name was changed to Savannah after Savannah, Georgia. Still, the fable about how Savannah got its name, featuring a 19th-century girl escaping death by covered wagon-trampling, is way more exciting than the town's actual origins.

When I was a kid living in that part of the country, it felt so lame. Not just Savannah, but all of Missouri, Kansas, Iowa, and Nebraska—every state that was near me. There was seemingly nothing exciting about that region of the world. No oceans, no mountains, just farms and rows of crops for miles. On television, you would see people living in big cities, leading a hustle-bustle life. Women would have a "little black dress" that they would go out in. Men would worry about picking up flowers and chocolates before courting their ladies. They would have to decide which restaurant to go to. Nothing could have been further from my reality back then. There weren't a whole lot of restaurants to choose from in Savannah, just a couple of fast food burger joints, a Pizza Hut and some local diners, none of which you would ever dress up for. There was really no place where wearing sweat pants would be frowned upon.

It was also literally impossible to go out and not run into someone you knew. No matter where you went... to the gas station, to the Pizza Hut, out for a walk, buying tampons at the drug store...anywhere you went, you would see someone you knew. Sometimes it was nice. You could always see a friendly face, and you never felt like a stranger. Sometimes it wasn't nice. Sometimes you would just want to leave the house, not brush your hair, run your errands, and come home without stopping to make small talk with every other person you saw.

Small town living didn't have a lot of class issues. Yeah, there were some rich kids and some poor kids, but the median was overwhelmingly the same. We all lived a pretty decent life back in the '80s. Not everyone wore

Jordache jeans every day, but almost everyone had at least one pair. No one drove a Bentley, but there weren't people living out in the streets, either. We all had roofs over our feathered hair and food in our stomachs.

The town wasn't crime-free, but there wasn't much crime to speak of. You could go anywhere and not lock your vehicle. During the harsh winter months, people did not even turn off their cars if they had to go into the grocery store. You would pass the parking lot and see the exhaust from dozens of empty cars as people shopped, not wanting to return to a freezing automobile.

Since it was such a tight-knit region, I would always get very anxious when I heard sirens, especially when there were a lot of sirens, like fire trucks, ambulances, and cop cars all responding to the same call. The bigger the noise, the more I would be worried that someone I knew might be involved. (I remember after a few months of living in Kansas City, when I had to pull over on the road to screaming emergency vehicles whizzing by me, I felt a sense of relief that I did not have to concern myself with the outcome of their destination. They were going somewhere in a big city where I knew very few people, and that comforted me in a weird way).

A friend of mine had an elderly aunt who would spend her days monitoring a police scanner. She knew what was going on in town as it happened. If there was ever any big commotion going in Savannah, we would give my friend's aunt a call and get the behind the scenes scoop. "Aunt Linda" was a one-woman TMZ of her day. And if you had a job within the city limits of Savannah, forget about playing hooky. If you called out of work, you needed to stay at home with your car securely in front of your house. If you were seen out and about looking happy and healthy on a "sick day," people would talk.

In fact, people would always talk about everything and everyone. Gossip was never in short supply. It was fun when it was juicy and about someone who got themselves in a world of trouble. It was awful when you were the one who got in trouble and were the target of the juicy gossip. I lived in Savannah prior to the Internet and social media. In a small town, word of mouth travels pretty fast even without technology. Who needs fiber optics when the morning gab fests over coffee in the diner could get any piece of good dirt around town in the speed of light?

It was hard to do things you weren't supposed to be doing in a small town, because the people that knew you also knew your parents. I would buy a pack of cigarettes at a convenience store when I was in my late teens/early twenties and ask the cashier not to tell my mom. The cashier would look at me and sigh, saying "Robin, you are an adult. You can smoke if you want to."

"Yeah, I know, but my mom already knew I came home drunk last night," I would reply. "I threw up a little next to her car. If she knew about the cigarettes too, she may lose respect for my life choices. Just please don't tell her. Okay?"

To some of the residents in my home town, Savannah was the entire universe. It was all some people had ever known. They assumed that the way folks in town conducted themselves was the way the world conducts itself. The lack of other cultures and people of different nationalities was not a real issue to the citizens of this small Missouri town. Big city problems were just that, stuff you saw on the news. I always thought that if the town collectively got together and decided to decree that the grass was blue and the sky was green, and as long as the majority of people bought into it, it would be considered true, in spite of the facts that proved otherwise.

When we first moved to Savannah we lived on a 40-acre farm. We only lived there for a few years. I was the ages of five to 10 years old during that time. In the country, one lives more of a "basic" life. In our first few months of living at the farmhouse, the indoor plumbing was not very functional. I remember having to pump water from a little well in the front of our house until the kitchen got modernized. You would literally have to prime the pump with stored water and pump and pump until the water came out. It was always kind of rusty and brown at first. You would have to keep pumping it until it became clear. I have always been a little grateful for sinks and running faucets from that experience.

We had plenty of livestock, including chickens, cattle, pigs, and one very mean horse. We butchered some of the chickens in our backyard. I have seen baby pigs being born at all hours of the day and night. A few times, it was in the freezing cold, and we had to wrap the teensy piglets in towels and put them under a makeshift heat lamp. I have watched lots of cows make the sweet bovine love. We would actually put the heifers in a pen with the bull. It was really more controlled animal rape to be technical. It's not pretty or politically correct; it is just how life is lived on a farm, raw and unfiltered.

My favorite animals back then were the cows. They were kind of like cats, but on larger scale; they did their own thing and did not bother you unless they were hungry. They could be silly, though, in their own way.

(My grandfather had a cow that would always get its head caught in a bucket of grain. The first few times it happen by accident, but eventually, my grandfather would purposely put out a bucket with a small amount of corn on the bottom. Like clockwork, "Brownie" would stick her face in, get her head caught, and swing it wildly until the bucket flew off, while my grandfather laughed the whole time). Cows are pretty nosy too. If there is a loud noise or something new to see, they would come around and stare at it for hours. Granted, the cows would never try to sit on your lap for a quick snuggle or a chin scratch, like a cat, but they are amiable and quirky creatures.

Chickens were the worst. They were gross and smelled awful. We had two types of chickens—the kind that laid eggs and the ones that you killed to eat, the "fryers." The "fryers" were uglier and more ill-mannered than the ones who laid the eggs. The "fryers" were bigger. Their combs, the red fleshy things on the top of their heads, were pinkish and flaccid, their feathers were whitish/yellow. The "layers" had more of a petite build and whiter feathers, and their combs were red and more erect, (no pun intended).They just looked prettier, although the whole lot of them were a bunch of assholes.

Our chicken coop was really disgusting. It was a stinky little shack with a dirt floor. I had to feed the chickens, and when you walked in with a bucket of grain they would go crazy. The birds would scurry to the two circular feeders in the center of the coop, some clucking and some flying (as much as chickens can fly). It would always stir up dust and feathers. They would clamor together and fight with one another to get close to the food. I hated those chickens with a passion.

While they were eating, I had to collect the eggs. Gathering eggs from chickens was another disgusting aspect of my chores. The eggs are not pretty and white like you see at the grocery store. By the time they make it into the egg cartons, they have been cleaned up, but most have some kind of poop on them at first. Both the eggs and the poop come from the back of a chicken, it is not a huge stretch to think that they will touch one another. So along with gathering eggs, I had to wash them later. (And if an egg broke while I was collecting them, the chickens would all gather around it and eat it like it was their last supper. Nasty little cannibals they were.)

As an adult, I was once offered chicken chitlins from a coworker at a company potluck. I had never had eaten chitlins before, and I am a big foodie. I am always game to try new things. I popped some into my mouth and almost instantly vomited. Apparently chitlins are just fried intestines, and it tasted like our chicken coop smelled. I gagged as loudly as one would who just mentally put chicken shit in their mouth. There was no time for discretion or being tactful around the person who was showing off her delicious handed-down family recipe. I spit it out while simultaneously retching. "Oh, dear God" I said while wiping the tears that were instantly pouring out of my eyes and trying to explain my reaction between heaves. "Seriously, it is not your cooking, I just grew up on a farm, and the taste of your food reminded me of the inside of a filthy chicken coop. Had I had a different upbringing, I would have thoroughly enjoyed your covered dish, I am sure."

Although I don't remember all of the farm animals, a few of them stand out in my memory. We once had a cow named Mrs. Moo. She was an old white cow. I really liked her. She had several calves while she lived on our farm. I remember the day that we sold her, my parents said that she was going to a feedlot for old cows. I felt sad to see her go, but thought that she would be happy around cows her own age. We had a lot of youthful cattle, and she probably was looking to enjoy her twilight years without being surrounded by all the current pasture hooligans, I decided. In hindsight, I am sure there was no such feedlot for old cows, and no sanctuary for bovine Nanas; Mrs. Moo probably met her demise shortly after being sold.

We also had a horse. She was a mare named Idget. She was the equivalent of the crotchety old man who always yells at the neighborhood kids for being on his lawn. We would isolate her from the rest of the animal population. My dad knew a guy with a Shetland pony named Tom. Sometimes we would keep Tom on our land and put him in the same section of pasture with Idget. Tom's hoofs were never clipped and were curly and stacked up on his feet. We never rode Tom, as he wasn't our pony and my dad used to say his feet probably hurt since his hooves weren't properly groomed.

I tried to ride Idget a few times. I liked horses, and she was really pretty. She hated to be ridden, though, and pulled out every evil trick in her equestrian arsenal to avoid doing any real work. She only wanted to eat grass and do nothing in her little corner of our farm. I remember once, my dad put me on her. I was riding bareback (meaning with no saddle) and just a lead rope (which wasn't reigns; she just had on a face halter that had a rope attached to it).While my dad was in the pasture with me, Idget behaved herself. My dad then told me to keep riding, and that he was going to work on the garden, which was maybe 40 yards away. He could still see me; it was just on the other side of a fence.

I continued to ride the horse, but as soon as my father's attention was diverted, Idget took advantage of the situation. I was scrawny for most of my childhood, so having a 40- or 50-pound kid on her back wasn't much of challenge for a full-sized horse. Idget took off running; she wouldn't stop. I pulled on the lead rope and took a fist of her mane and yelled "Whoah!!!", but that didn't work. I remember seeing Dad look up from garden. The rake was still in his hand, and his face was terrified. At that point, I changed my verbal command to, "Dad, help!!!" The horse continued to run, until she got to the fence, made a dead stop, put her head down, and started eating the grass that was growing tall nearby. At which point, I did not stop. I slid down her neck and popped my elbow on the gate. My dad, who must have sprinted from the garden, was suddenly there, grabbing me by the armpit and pulling me up to safety. Although, I have gone onto ride many other horses since that day, that was last time I rode Idget.

We had a lot of farm dogs, too. Our first dog was named Daisy. She was a Norwegian Elkhound. Although, I am more of a cat person, I cannot say enough good things about that breed of dog. They are very sweet and gentle creatures. Daisy was great with kids; she was always up to playing with us and was never aggressive. Her mouth was turned slightly upward, and she always looked like she was smiling. We once saw that Daisy was keeping to herself in the doghouse. She had something that was she licking between her paws and did not want to be distracted. When my mom approached the dog, she realized it was a tiny new-born rabbit, still alive. Daisy was mothering it as if it were her baby puppy. That dog could have made the little bunny a quick in-between-meal snack, but she did not. She was protecting it and keeping it warm and safe from the outside world.

We also had a little pig named Pig Pig. He started out as any other piglet, just one of the babies from the many litters we had from our sows, but then his intestines started coming out of his butt. We had to put a butt plug in it and keep him isolated from the other pigs. Pig Pig became really friendly, almost like a dog. He would follow us around. His butt plug-thingy eventually fell off, but occasionally it would rub against me and gross me out. I would try to avoid his back end most of the time. He got too big to be a pet; we eventually sold him as well.

There was another pig named Petunia. She just wandered into our farm one day, like a stray dog. We asked around, but no one was missing a full-sized black and white pig. We kept her, fed her and she eventually gave us several litters of pigs. It wasn't until a decade later that my father told me that we had actually slaughtered and ate Petunia. I was in my twenties when he admitted that, and she had long since been digested by then. I was shocked at first, but what are you going to do? Eventually you find out childhood truths…There is no Santa Claus, your parents are just as human as anyone else and you unknowingly ate your pets. It is all just life's lessons for farm children.

My parents divorced when I was 10 years old. When they split up, my mother, brother, and I moved into town. Life in the city limits of Savannah was a lot more fun. I had more independence. This was when you could let your kids ride their bikes everywhere without fear that they would be snatched. I would ride to my friends' houses. Our days would consist of walking to the grocery store, riding our bikes to the TG&Y, and going to the swimming pool in the summer time. It was a pretty good life for a kid. A 40-acre farm gave you a lot of room to play and provided animals to get in dysfunctional relationships with, but once I got older, I became a lot more social and valued living in town. Unlike Oliver the farmer from the television show "Green Acres," farm living was not the life for me.

When I was in high school, I worked at the town's bowling alley with my best friend, Tina. We were the waitresses/fry cooks. I think that job was probably the hardest job for the least amount of pay that I have ever worked. I did not know any better as it was my first job. I was responsible for feeding the bowling crowd, waiting on them, cooking their food, making them nervous when my shaking hands poured steaming coffee into their cups, and cleaning the kitchen thoroughly at the end of the night (which included straining two giant vats of scalding-hot grease). I made tips, but most people just slipped me a few quarters—I guess because I was a teenager and it was bowling alley food.

Tina and I got to know a bunch of guys in their twenties who would come in to bowl. (It was also the only place in town where you could buy beer on a Sunday. It used to be that in the state of Missouri, you could sell only beer with an alcohol content of 3.2 percent on the Lord's Day. I think it was in the scriptures" "On the seventh day, thou shall rest and drink really watered-down, shitty beer.") The older guys would give Tina and I lots of attention and could sometimes be persuaded to buy a stash of alcohol for all of our friends. We had fun with a couple of them, but never got serious with any of those guys. It also was not easy to really go out after you got off work; you smelled like the giant vat of hot grease that you had just strained.

There were two little old ladies who used to always come in for coffee, and they once called Tina's Mom to tell her that we were hanging out with older guys at work. Neither Tina nor I got in any trouble from the phone call. I think her Mom was amazed that those old ladies were that nosy and meddling. Plus, when we agreed to work at a bowling alley, both of our mothers knew that Rhodes scholars did not hang out there; the clientele was made up of guys who liked to bowl and drink beer. We both only lasted a year working there. It was fun, but when you get the call from the Hardees in town asking you to join their team, you can't turn that offer down. That gig comes with a brown polyester uniform and a hat.

I do not make it back to Savannah as often as I would like to. I have taken my kids back there a time or two. They love it. To them, going from hot and sticky old Florida to cooler and greener Missouri is always a great vacation. I still get together with my old high school friends. We all have kids now and let them play and get to know each other while we laugh and talk about days gone by. I love my friends and my memories of that crazy little spot on the map where I spent my formative years. It made me who I am today. It made me a Savage.

Chapter Twelve
The Land Sharks

I have been a runner for most of my life. I started participating in Fun Runs in the early 80's on the weekends and during the summers I spent with my father after my parents got divorced. My Dad moved around the Midwest due to his job, but he was always within a four-hour radius from me in Missouri. Weekends with my Dad were never lazy. We camped or swam or ran, plus he wasn't much of a TV watcher. He could only get local channels on the one tiny TV set that he had, so running would beat watching a test pattern or a fuzzy local news station.

I was 11 or 12 years old at the time. I thought the running itself was physically painful, but I liked the camaraderie of the races. Everyone was always nice, and you got bananas and bagels at the end of the run. People would volunteer to work booths that offered water or Gatorade during the race. The runners were encouraged to just drink the water and throw the little paper cups on the ground. As a kid, getting permission to publicly litter was awesome! The same volunteers would sweep the streets afterwards. Everyone cheered for you. The spectators didn't discriminate; it didn't matter if you were the first guy who crossed the finish line, or were dead last. You always heard, "Keep it up! You're doing great!" Fun runs were—and still are—really just a couple of skipped showers and a hit of acid away from hippy love-ins.

My Dad was never very social, so it was unusual for him to be around that many people at once—although maybe since everyone was running, it didn't leave time for tedious small talk. Most of the runners were very enthusiastic. There was no stereotypical runner. They all varied in age, creed, color, and body type.   I still remember how my Dad would always muse, when we met old people who were still running their hearts out, "Look at them go. That's so neat."

Running was also an activity that just my Dad and I did. No one else ran with us. I think the physical pain associated with running may have played a role in that. We would have matching shirts from the event. Like most Americans, I have always had a million T-shirts in my wardrobe, but the apparel I got from the runs was always my favorite because not everyone could get it. TG&Y didn't sell "Run For The Hill Of It, Salina KS 1983" T-shirts; you had to earn them.

I continued to run in high school and joined the track team. Again, I didn't run for the love of running; I ran because it was literally the only sport at which I didn't COMPLETELY suck. I wasn't great, but I wasn't as embarrassingly klutzy as when I played the sports that required coordination and natural athletic ability, neither of which I had. So Track and Field was it for me. I could be part of the team without having to throw a ball, catch a ball, or have another human depend on me during the actual competition. I would run the one-mile or two-mile race during a track meet. I would either lose the race entirely by coming in last place, or I would win a few races. I hardly ever placed in any order other than first or last. (I think that would later become a metaphor for my life.)

Still, I kept running, even in my roaring twenties. After nights of drinking and eating too much, I would still manage to lace up my shoes and get moving that next day…sometimes. In hindsight, it may have been a bad thing. I would be having fun the night before and think to myself, "I need to make this my last beer." Or, "I ate way too much. I should stop shoveling this food into my face." Then, a little voice in the back of my head would say, "No, you're good. Just run it off tomorrow." I most assuredly never ran it all off. Often, I wouldn't even follow through with the run, or if I did run, it was never hard enough to erase the previous night. (There probably weren't enough miles in Kansas City to do that.) I would usually start out running, then walk, then go home and decide that the next time I went out I wouldn't overindulge. It wasn't great exercise, but it was enough to keep my muscles from completely atrophying during that time of my life.

When I got into my thirties, I didn't drink nearly as much, and running got to be its own social outlet. I had friends from work with whom I would run. We would even sign up for Fun Runs like the ones I participated in as a kid. It was at this point that I decided to pursue a life's goal of running a marathon. I told one of my running buddies about it, and we decided that we would take on this task together. We even joined a Runner's Club. It met early mornings on Saturdays, which—as it never would have when I was in my twenties— actually prevented me from overeating or even drinking at all on Friday nights. My mindset was totally different at that point. I would think, "I have the Runner's Club in the morning. I can't be hung over. I will throw up or pass out, and it will make me look like a pussy. I am going to try to get to sleep early." If only I could have applied that same wisdom a decade earlier in my life.

Again, when I joined the Runner's Club, I was reminded of the gentleness of the collective group of people who are runners. At the time, I was one of the youngest in the group, the mean age was 40-ish, and not everyone was in great shape, but they all had great attitudes. The program was well-organized and laid out a plan that made it helpful to actually achieve running 26.2 miles. As with any big undertaking, when you run a marathon, you have to start out slow. You run smaller distances at first, and then you eventually start running the longer courses (once your body acclimates to the voluntary pounding you are subjecting it to). In the thick of the program, on our long-distance Saturdays, we would run 15 to 20 miles, and then every other Saturday we would run 10 miles. The 10-mile runs started to become my favorite. My body was getting strong enough to handle running for that long. Anything over that amount was really painful, and anything under it seemed wimpy. (Side note: I can only run three or four miles now without throwing up or passing out. Eleven years and two kids later, even driving ten miles is really painful.)

The Runner's Club people kept talking about the importance of good running shoes. They said to have a few pairs and alternate them. As per usual, I figured I knew better and didn't want to waste my money, so I stuck with my same shoes. At a certain point, I totally blew out my right knee. This also came on the heels of my husband having the "baby" talk with me. He had decided that it was "now or never" to try to reproduce. We were both in our thirties, and neither of us was getting any younger. (Bear in mind, these were the same exact words I said to him when I turned thirty, at which time he had assured me we still had a few good years left.) When he pressed the issue of starting a family, I reiterated that I wanted a baby. I always had, but I had already devoted six months of my life, including six months of well-behaved Friday nights, to this goal. I promised him we would start on the baby-making right after I ran my marathon. (I probably would shower first.) So when my knee gave out, I was leery about getting it examined. I was worried that the doctor would tell me not to run the race, and I did not want to postpone starting a family even more, until the knee healed and I could complete the marathon. But since I am never very good at following through with tasks, I worried that if I didn't run this race, I probably wouldn't ever run a marathon.

Instead of going to the doctor, I bought a new pair of shoes, strapped in, and finished the race. It was not pretty; my knee started hurting around mile five. I ran the marathon in over six hours, and as my husband would later point out, the race officials were putting away the orange street cones and cleaning up the race course when I made it through the finish line. But I made it, and that is what counts. I had actually accomplished a life goal and could scratch one thing off my Bucket List.

Although I haven't run a marathon since and probably never will again, I still run. Even though it is still physically painful, it always makes me feel better and clears my head. It is still sometimes hard for me to get motivated to run, but I am always glad afterwards. I do find that I am not nearly as disciplined when I run by myself. I will stop and walk when no one is running with me.

I recently found out that a friend of mine is in a running club that meets during the week. It is very well organized and for people with race goals. I don't have race goals, but I wanted to be a part of a group to push myself harder than when I run alone. I asked her if anyone would object if I ran with them, and she said it was an open group that meets at the YMCA.

Once more, I found myself in the company of lovely people who shared a love of running. They named the running group the "Land Sharks." We are all adults, most with children of our own, and we are all associated with a group called the Land Sharks. A few people even sport Land Shark T-shirts. Since my affection for runners has always been very high and I invited myself into the group, I don't feel right making fun of that name, but unfortunately as a comedian, I am obligated to do it.

For one, sharks don't run or live on land. If they did, wouldn't they just flop around? Runners aren't intense or intimidating like sharks. We are all running with ear buds and MP3 players strapped to our biceps. Not many sharks are secretly listening to Katy Perry, but claim it is Zeppelin. I don't understand the significance of the name. There are no land creatures that we submerse in water for the sake of being mascots, like sea tigers or pond lions. Why did adults feel the need to name this group? Was "Wednesday Morning Running Club at the Y" taken?

I constantly amuse myself and annoy my family by referring to this club. "Don't forget after I drop you kids off at school, I have to meet with the Land Sharks this morning," I tell my children every Wednesday. I even use the same shark hand gesture Steve Martin used when he sang "Mac the Knife"...."Land Sharks...Grrrr." My kids usually ignore me and tell me they don't care that I am a part of the Land Sharks. I will sometimes break into a song that sounds like the "Jet Song" from the musical "West Side Story": "When you're a Land Shark, you're a Land Shark all the way; from your first cigarette, to your last dying day."

"That's stupid, Mom, You can't smoke and be a runner," they tell me.

"Dun Don Dun Don... Land Shark!" I say as I make my shark hand gesture.

I hope to one day complete a Fun Run with my children, just like I did with my father. I won't ever push either of my kids into it, though. I think you either are a runner, or you aren't. Until then, you can see me on the open road, running at a moderate pace, listening to Lynyrd Skynyrd (Beyonce) and still regretting my food choices from the night before. You can't stop me. I will always be moving forward, never back, just like a shark...a land shark.

Chapter Thirteen
The Boys of Hogwarts

When I was first introduced to JK Rowling's Harry Potter, I was in my early thirties. I did not have kids then, and could not have cared less about children's fiction. I had an English friend who did not have kids either, but was a Harry Potter fanatic. She said the Harry Potter books were incredible, and that the movie (there was only one Harry Potter movie out at the time) was just as great. My friend was not much of a reader, so she listened to books on tape. She offered to lend me the tapes from the first book of the series, "Harry Potter and The Sorcerer's Stone."

The thought of listening to a book on tape piqued my interest. I have better success at jogging when I listen to music, but I had never tried an audio novel before. When I run without any sort of distraction, I tend to focus on the pain and boredom of forcing myself to run. This was in the early 2000s, so I strapped on my always stylish, five-pound cassette recorder with its giant earphones and took off. My friend could not have been more right. I was instantly hooked. I wanted to save Harry from the awful Muggles. I was captivated by Diagon Alley. I wanted an invisibility cloak like the one Harry had inherited from his father, but most importantly I fell madly in love with Ron Weasley. (Not a romantic love, as he is a fictional child and that would have been creepy, but an instant favorite character kind of love.) That little redhead had me from the first meeting at Platform Nine and Three-Quarters. I even love the actor, Rupert Grint, who plays Ron in the movies. He is absolutely adorable, especially in the first film—he was so little, so cute, and so ginger.

I could relate to Harry, because I kind of adopted my best friend's family when I was a kid, too. While my own family was alive and well and not at all killed by Voldemort or his army of Death Eaters, we were all separate from one another. My Dad had lived elsewhere since I was ten years old, my brother had his own life while in high school and moved to California after graduating, and my Mom worked nights. The Jacobs family was my Weasleys. But even though I was more like Harry, I rooted for Ron. Ron was kind of the Charlie Brown of Wizards. He could never really win. He was lost in the crowd within his own family. Hogwarts didn't really have huge expectations for him either; he was just another Weasley boy. When Ron finally found a best friend and started making a life of his own, Harry always got all the attention. The irony was that all Harry ever wanted was to have a family like the Weasleys. Ah, JK, you know how to weave a good tale.

After listening to the first book on tape, I bought and read the actual book and then bought and read the next three books. At that time, the last three books had not yet been written. As the series progressed, the books became bigger (literally) and the hype surrounding them became insane. I also bought the first movie, and then the next three as soon as they came out.

When the seventh and last book was unveiled, there were a lot of rumors that many of the characters were going to be killed off. At the time, everyone was speculating that it would be Harry. I knew it would not. That would have been too "on the nose." I knew that Harry would be spared. He was the hero, and the series was named for him, so I was certain that he was safe. But I was scared for my little coppertop, my Ron. I was worried that he would have been the one to get the ax (or the wand, more likely). It would have been plausible. Ron could have sacrificed himself for Harry. He could have died a hero's death, or at least that was my irrational fear in the summer of '07. I literally read the 800-plus-page book in one weekend because I had to make sure that Ron was not one of the doomed characters. Had Ron died, it would have been a heart breaker. He would have been mourned, but as the years went by, the memory of him would have faded. A Weasley child may have been named after him, like a nephew or something, but his unsung life would have been the real tragedy. Thank God he lived, and I did not have to experience the bereavement that comes with losing a fictional character. I don't have the emotional capacity for that.

I obviously have a weird obsession with this series, but I keep it in check. I don't go to conventions or dress-up like a witch. Okay, I may have thought about getting a life-sized poster of Ron a few times or rehearsed my "I am just buying this for a 'friend'" retort for when the clerk at the bookstore would inevitably have seen me whisper to the rolled-up picture. "We'll be home soon. Sshh, you're safe with Mama now." But that never happened, or at least, it cannot be proven.

The closest I ever came to any type of "wizarding" convention was when I was asked to perform stand up comedy at a Dr. Who singles mixer. At first I was worried this would be a bad fit, since I was neither single nor a Dr. Who fan. The guy who booked me asked me if I could refrain from telling a few bawdier jokes, as he felt that the attendees of this mixer were all very innocent and it would make them uncomfortable. He was so wrong.

Although, the mixer had been advertised as Dr. Who-themed, it was more like a nerdy role-playing free-for-all. People were dressed not only like the cast from Dr. Who, but also as Harry Potter and characters from "The Lord of the Rings trilogy," and I think there were even a few Trekkies represented as well. Granted, there was a definite geeky ambience in the room, but there wasn't much innocence from that group. Most of the women were dressed like slutty versions of the characters that they were portraying.

The act that was performing before me was a council of lady "Whovians." I am not sure what their purpose was, but the group consisted of three women dressed up in costumes and taking questions from the audience about which fictional characters they would have sex with. It was weird. I didn't really care about any of it and was starting to mentally put back into my set all the jokes I had taken out. Nothing in my act came close to being as shocking as the girl in a Tardis costume, with her breasts almost fully exposed. (Phone booths don't have tits. It made no sense.)

Then I heard someone question the panel about what Ron and Hermoine's intimate life would be like. I was not happy. I wanted to scream, "Shut up, you whores!

You don't talk about Ron Weasley like that. I love him!"
I didn't, though. If people want to live in a delusional
world, worrying about make believe personas, there is
nothing I can do about it but judge.

If I ever did take time to further explore my Harry
Potter obsession, I would write to JK Rowling and tell
her to stop trying to bring these characters back to life in
one form or another. She should let them rest in the
pages of her seven wonderful books. After the last book
was published, JK announced that she regretted having
Ron and Hermione get together at the end of the series.
She said that in hindsight, she should have had Harry and
Hermione marry. Give me a damn break! So Ron was
just going to get the short end of the stick for his entire
life? He wasn't even going to be with the girl he adored?
Harry would have taken Ron's true love, even after all
the years that Ron was his relegated side kick? Why do
you hate Ron, JK? Why?

It ended the way it should have ended. Maybe there
was chemistry between Harry and Hermione, but putting
them together would have disconnected both of them
from the whole Weasley clan. That is really all Harry
ever wanted—to be a part of a family, to be accepted and
loved. Ginny made him a bona fide Weasley, not
Hermione   Had Harry and Hermione gotten married,
they would have been a well-off wizarding couple living
in a flat in London, like yuppies—or wuppies in their
case. They would not have had children. They would
have had the best of intentions to reproduce, but their
careers in magic would have gotten in the way. Yeah,
they would still have seen Ron at reunions or at various
Hogwarts Alumni functions, but it would have not been
the same. Ron would have continued to drift, drinking

too much butterbeer, having a different witch on his arm every night, and never settling down or finding true happiness.

Most recently, Rowling wrote a short story that follows up with Hogwarts Alumni as if they were in their 30s and reuniting at a Quiddich match (Quiddich is the sport that they play in the book with flying brooms and varying sized balls). The short story is written in the voice of Rita Skeeter, a sleazy tabloid-type journalist within the series, so it shows all of our favorites in a negative light. While it can be argued that since Rita Skeeter is the one who is telling the story, that none of what was portrayed was true for the characters in the story. I still don't like it. I want Rowling to stop writing about Harry Potter and his friends. That entire story needs to walk out in the sunset with dignity, but Rowling keeps bringing it back like an annoying house guest that left, forgot their purse, returned and then sticks around to chat longer.

Even though I have mixed emotions about the future of the series, I knew many years ago—after getting hooked on the series when I read "Harry Potter and the Sorcerer's Stone,"—that I would someday introduce my future children to the wonderful world of Hogwarts and all the magic that surrounded it. Eventually, when I had kids, they went through all kinds of phases in their entertainment choices. As toddlers, their favorite television shows were "Dora the Explorer" and "Diego," and the books were Dr. Seuss and the like. When they got older, I read them some books by Judy Blume, who had been my favorite author when I was in school. It was the kids who brought home the "Magic Tree House" series, which was new to me and fun to read with them. I never pushed Harry Potter on them at an early age. I did not want it to make them fearful of losing their parents or think that the book was too scary.

My son got sick when he was eight years old—not a serious illness, just a bad flu that kept him in bed for three or four days. He was in one of those moods that kids get in when they are not feeling well. He wanted his Mama close, and Mama was going insane after the third day of non-stop "SpongeBob SquarePants" episodes on the television. I thought this might be a good time to introduce him to Harry Potter. Joel was familiar with the books and movies. Most kids are. He had even tried reading "Harry Potter and the Sorcerer's Stone" once, but it was a little too advanced for him at that time. I started reading it to him that afternoon. He loved it. After he felt better, he watched the four movies that we had at home. Later, I got him the last four movies for his birthday.

I am noticing that as my son gets older, it is harder to relate to him as I do to my daughter. My son and I do not paint our toenails together, and I do not borrow his necklaces for big comedy shows or ask him which lipstick I should wear like I do with my girl. My son likes football, but aside from me talking to him about how I used to go the Kansas City Chiefs games back in the day, I cannot relate to him about sports that much. Harry Potter has become our thing, our bond that we have in common. Joel has gotten older, and his reading skills have improved. He reads the books on his own now, but we still get together and read one out loud sometimes. We have watched several of the movies together. We have also gotten into various Harry Potter discussions, like who is smarter, Harry or Hermione? (I say Hermione, but he contends that she was only smarter when they were younger. (I say that she has always been smarter; Harry just had extra magic help.) Joel told me that he was the most sad when Fred Weasley died. He also felt that Snape was the true hero of the book for protecting Harry, even though James Potter had been cruel to Snape at times and was in love with Harry's mother. I am always amazed at Joel's observations and insights.

I like watching my son discover the magic of the wizarding world, as well as the magic of reading. I only feel bad that Ron Weasley has once again lost out to another boy. Ron still has my literary affection, but my son will always have my real-life heart.

Chapter Fourteen
Can I Get A Second Opinion?

I use social media quite a bit. I am on Facebook to promote shows, keep up with the comedy scene, and try to provide witty posts every now and again to remind my Facebook friends why I am a comedian. Social media also allows me to keep up with classmates I vaguely remember from high school, random people I met once at a comedy show, and a few relatives with whom I have only an acquaintance-type relationship. I have my nose in my laptop, reading up on their lives, while my own children are growing, playing and laughing around me.

I think social media is the closest outlet we will ever have to reading someone else's mind. There are some folks who use Facebook to express every opinion and emotion they have ever had on any given subject. There have been times that I have read a post that was so personal and weird, it actually caused me to look away from the keyboard in discomfort. I think that instead of asking the question, "What's on your mind?" as a status prompt, Facebook should warn, "What do you want to share with everyone on your Friends List today? Remember, your Mom can read this. No takesy-backseys."

I have come to the realization that knowing this much about other people's inner thoughts is very powerful. I know some individuals who have had their whole day ruined by someone else's posts. I used to be mildly amused by folks getting caught up in using a free computer application when no one has forced them to do so. Over the years, though, social media has turned into a revolution. Companies monitor their employees with it, it was responsible for the whole Arab Spring, and there are many privacy questions surrounding the way our personal data is being collected and used. Still, even with all this controversy, millions of people—myself included—sign in every day to look at the endless string of comments, pictures, and videos that people post.

I can handle opinions that differ from mine. If a person has a logical, fact-based reason to feel a certain way, I can respect it. I can even deal with opinions that are not fact-based, providing that they are well thought out rather than just knee-jerk, emotional reactions to someone or something. It is the sheer ignorance-filled and spiteful posts that drive me insane. Take for instance, people's opinion on music. My kids love pop music. They listen to the Top 40 stations and know all the current "It" stars. My daughter is a big fan of Taylor Swift. She knows all of the lyrics to "TSwift's" songs. As a Mom, I think Taylor Swift makes a pretty good role model. She writes her own music, overcame being bullied, and made the transition from country music singer to pop sensation. Swift has never been publicly drunk or high. No paparazzi pics of her entering a vehicle with her bare hoo-hoo showing have ever been published. She has never fondled a sleazy singer with a foam finger during a live performance. Granted, the young blonde has had a lot of boyfriends, but that's what your twenties are for. Besides, there is no solid proof that she is actually sleeping with any of her suitors—which may explain the short relationships and break-up songs. Her music appeals to young people, especially young girls. It is marketed to them, listened to by them, and bought by them. She is a voice for her generation.

It irritates me when I read posts by grown adults insulting these young artists with hateful talk. Granted, despising your kids' music is a rite of passage of sorts. Pop music will always be about the newest generation. It's about expression and rebellion and how this latest flock of humans interprets the world around them. Adults need to stop bitching about how today's music isn't anything like the music of their era. It is not, nor is it supposed to be. Every generation is different. We all have a different look and a different style. We learn different lessons. It is called life. We are young for just a moment in time, and one day we fondly look back and say, "What was I thinking wearing THAT outfit?"

When I was in high school, it was the big-haired bands that outraged the grownups. The dudes with eye-liner, tight pants, and Aquanet-coiffed manes gave our elders fits. In hindsight, they did look pretty ridiculous. In foresight, those rockers all morphed into old women as they aged. No other generation of musicians seemed to be as enamored of long flowing scarves as some of the 80's rock bands were.

I remember that in early 2002, my grandmother and her husband came out to my house for a visit. The United States was fresh off the September 11th terrorist attacks, and emotions were still pretty raw for everyone. My grandmother's husband, Ed, was then in his late seventies. He began a diatribe about The Beatles. He literally blamed the state of the early 21st century politics on the 1960's Fab Four (not failed U.S. foreign policy, political corruption, or oil production, but the British musical group). I nearly spit out my drink (probably beer).

"You don't like The Beatles?" I asked. "Seriously? I have NEVER heard of anyone NOT liking The Beatles. They paved the way for so many modern musicians."

"That's exactly my point, Robin," he told me. "They came in with their music and hair, and just look at the problems we have today."

"Seriously?" I repeated. "You think The BEATLES are to blame for terrorism? The BEATLES??? John, George, Paul, and Ringo? Those Beatles? The ones who were famous in the 1960s? You realize that two of them aren't even alive anymore, right?"

That said, I was watching WWE with my son one night. WWE is "professional" wrestling. My son loves it. He knows all the wrestlers' names and the ongoing feuds. He has favorite wrestlers and ones he hates. He even knows who their wives and girlfriends are (some of their "ladies" wrestle as well). My son is enveloped in the antics and drama of this program. WWE is his "Real Housewives" series.

The fight we were watching was something of a grudge match. (I later found out that most of these fights have some sort of revenge thread throughout them, again much like the "Real Housewives" shows). One wrestler had stolen another wrestler's life savings, which had been contained in a flashy briefcase labeled "Money Bank." From what I could gather, the wrestler whose money had been stolen was a good guy and therefore, my son liked him. The wrestler who had stolen the money was, apparently, a wrestling villain; hence my son passionately disliked that guy. I hate to engage in victim-blaming, but had the good guy wrestler just kept his loot in mutual funds, a credit union, or even a discreet wallet, none of this would ever have happened. I am not saying you are "asking for trouble" by putting all your money in a shiny container whose label clearly reveals its contents, but be aware, it will arouse curiosity.

So, we watched the fight. My son's eyes lit up and were glued to the television set. He cheered every time the good guy got in his licks. He groaned and yelled when the bad guy was leading, and just when it seemed that the good guy was going to lose, he ended up winning in the end. It was a nail-biter. There was a lot of trash talk, body slams, and illegal use of folding chairs.

As a stand up and an adult who has actually read a book in the last 15 years, I so wanted to make fun of it. Not in front of my son, of course, but I couldn't wait to go online and hit up the social media sites. The snarky Facebook posts were just crashing into my head: "Watched WWE tonight; saw more spandex, glitter and muscles than in a gay bar," "Watching professional wrestling is like watching a soap opera, but with better acting and less believable bitch slapping," and "WWE is the cubic zirconia of sports. It only fools the people who don't know any better." Then I got to thinking: Isn't this what irritates me about pop music being ridiculed? Aren't I being judgmental this time? The WWE isn't targeted to suburban white women in their forties. The WWE does not conduct market research to find out what imported wine most wrestling fans enjoy. No network executive is worried about whether "WWE Smackdown" will steal viewers from "Downton Abbey" if they air in the same time slot. WWE appeals to kids, especially little boys and adults who don't understand the "Downton Abbey" reference.

I think this is the problem with the world in general. We have lost all tolerance for people who are not exactly like us. There seems to be no room for differences or opposing points of view. If we have an opinion about a certain song or television show or movie or political view, we only listen to the people who agree with us. We seem to have lost any type of respect for any perspective other than our own. Social media exacerbates this type of situation by acting as an outlet for us to shout out our opinions. It's all "your side" or "my side." ...black or white. The only shades of gray these days are reserved for rough and kinky sex.

I think everyone is guilty of it. Leftist Liberals hate the Right Wing Christians, Right Wing Christians hate the Muslims, and the Muslims seemingly hate everyone but other Muslims. I realize that everyone is entitled to their opinion, but can't we just remember that everyone else is entitled to their opinion too? They say opinions are like assholes—everyone has one. But do we all have to act like one?

Chapter Fifteen
Mean Raw Bean

Before we had children, my husband and I took a trip to Switzerland. We ate at a restaurant attached to our hotel. The waiter was an interesting young man who spoke eight—that's right—eight languages and held several degrees, including a Masters, but was still relegated to serving drunken, loud Americans like my husband and me. He took us down to the restaurant's basement and showed us its enormous wine cellar. There was a giant Vikings table in a banquet room. As adults in our thirties at the time, my husband and I pretended to be Vikings, yelling at one another from opposite ends of the table in "funny" accents that I am sure weren't Swiss, Swedish, or Norwegian, just drunken American. This waiter, who was far more educated than both of us, laughed at our antics because serving us was his livelihood.

I only know English. I took French in high school. The only phrases that I ever gleaned translate to:

"Hi, my name is Robin, and you?"

"I am going to the beach, and you?"

"I am going to the hospital, and you?"

Stateside and years later, I once took my son shopping for summer shoes. He was five years old at the time. He had outgrown all his sandals and flip-flops. We went to a local Bealls store. Bealls is kind of like TJ Maxx or Ross. It sells discounted clothes, shoes, and home furnishings. The store was in my neighborhood, which is culturally diverse, but by no means exclusively Hispanic. None of the clerks at this particular store spoke any English. Since I fancy myself as worldly, I figured this would not be a problem. How hard would it be to ask where the little boys' shoes were while standing in a clothing store that sells shoes? Apparently, it was pretty difficult. The first sales lady had no clue what I was asking her. "Me no Ingles," she said, and waved over a second sales lady.

The second lady came over. I assumed she was the bilingual one of the group. No such luck. I had to pull out all the Spanish I knew, which is really just a few words that stuck in my brain from my children's "Dora the Explorer" years.

"Nino needs shoes," I told her, pointing to my son's feet.

"Ah, si," she said, staring at me blankly.

We stood there staring at each other.

"Nino, shoes," I repeated, pointing to my son's feet again.

"Ah, shoes," she replied. Then she pointed to the giant racks of shoes in back of the store, which I had already seen and looked through—only to find that that they held only adult shoes. There were no children's shoes and certainly no flip-flops.

"Yes, shoes," I acknowledged. "But I need nino shoes. Shoes for ninos."

"Ah, si shoes," she said yet again, pointing to the same shoe rack.

My son was looking up at her with his big blue eyes. He was right at the age where he no longer threw temper tantrums. I started getting frustrated and wanted to stamp my feet and yell, "This conversation is going nowhere!" I didn't, though. I had to show my son I was at least at his maturity level.

"Never mind," I told the sales lady. "Let me look around some more. Gracias."

I continued to look around the store and finally stumbled upon a section of socks and leggings next to the shoe racks. On the bottom shelf, I noticed a small selection of children's slip-on shoes. My son picked out a pair of bright blue Crocs that had the Chicago White Sox logo on them. (He never really knew who the White Sox were until then. I just told him they were baseball shoes). I left the store grumbling to myself: "This is still America. They couldn't have hired at least one person who spoke fucking English?" I kind of hated myself for feeling like that. I felt small-minded, but then again, should it have been that hard to ask for little boys' shoes in an American store?

Last year, a young family moved in next door to us. Initially I thought they were Hispanic or Latino. I heard them speaking to one another in a language that I assumed was Spanish. It was not that difficult an assumption to make since many of my other neighbors are Hispanic or Latino and we live in Tampa, Florida. Once I met these neighbors, I realized that the small family of three consisted of a man, who spoke only Italian; his wife, the mother, who is Cuban and spoke Spanish, Italian, and a little English; and their young daughter, who was then in kindergarten and spoke all three languages.

As I got to know my neighbors, I grew to really like them. The little girl, Deanna, and my daughter, Katie, became friends. Although Deanna could speak English, it was still a bit broken. She and her family called my daughter Katie "Kaley." At first Katie was polite about it. I think she kept hoping that the neighbors would eventually figure out that "Kaley" is not her name. (They never have, and Katie hates it.) My husband and I tried to explain to her that they were not being intentionally rude. "They speak a different language," I once told her. "They are not calling you 'Kaley' to make fun of you. That is just how they speak. They call me 'Rah-Beeen.' It is just their accent. They aren't purposefully calling me a raw bean." And "Kaley" was actually a better name than what they called my son, Joel. He was always referred to as "Kaley's Brother." At least "Kaley" was given a name and not just a description.

When we met the next-door neighbors, it was the middle of spring. At the time, my kids were attending a Charter School in a bad area of town . (I think I may be the only parent who actually had my kids bussed into a shitty area of town from the suburbs, rather than the other way around.) The school was really good, though. It was a math and science charter school. Plus, the schools in our area had been rezoned, and had I just let my kids attend their assigned public schools, they would eventually have gone to a middle school that was awful.

In the meantime, a brand-new charter school had been built in our area. It also specialized in math and science. The commute time and cost of gas to send the kids to the same type of school in the 'hood' were just killing us, so we decided to send them to the new, closer school. I had told Erin, Deanna's mother, about it in hopes of getting other kids in our sub-division to go to the new school as well.

I registered my kids for the new school that spring. I gave Erin the charter school's website address and told her to check it out. I hadn't heard back on the subject when, in mid-summer, she came knocking on my door. Erin had decided to send Deanna to the charter school and needed help filling out the forms. She could speak English fairly well, but struggled to read and write it, so I helped her complete all the necessary forms and faxed them over from my home fax machine. I figured that since it was a new school, getting accepted and enrolled would not be a problem.

On the day before the school year started, I took my kids to the school for the open house. Just as we were walking back to our car from the new building, Erin drove up in a panic. "Rahhh Beeen, they don't have the papers I filled out," Erin yelled out her car window.

"What? I faxed them over myself!" I exclaimed, starting to get concerned. I have this knack of somehow, some way fucking everything up I touch.

"I know. I tell them," Erin told me. "They don't see my name in computer. Can you help me talk to them, Rahhh Beeen? My English isn't so good."

"Of course, I can," I said, praying to God that this was not my fault.

We made our way back into the school and went to the front office. It was jam-packed with people asking the front desk ladies all sorts of questions. I can understand that after a while, it could be frustrating for the school's staff. It was a new year in a brand-new school. A lot of people had a lot of issues. After a long wait, it was our turn. The receptionist saw my neighbor returning and looked visibly irritated. I recognized that look. It was the same look I had had when I was at Bealls talking to the Hispanic sales associate. That same look made Erin shrink back and step aside so I could get closer to the counter.

This time, though, I felt bad for the person who could not speak the language. Erin had been trying to learn English to the best of her ability. She was also being a Mom and a wife and had a job that she went to every day. I had heard her switch back and forth from speaking Spanish and Italian without missing a beat, but today she was dealing with people who only knew one language.

"Hi, these folks are my neighbors. I am going to be helping them out, today." I said to the receptionist, smiling brightly at her, pointing to Erin and Deanna and silently hoping I could deflect the woman's sour puss attitude. "She downloaded and filled out the registration forms a month or so ago. I even faxed it over to the number on the application."

"Yes. I know, but she is not in our system. I have looked several times," the front desk lady said haughtily.

"Well, what can we do going forward?" I inquired, using my best customer service voice. "Is it too late to get her daughter registered?"

The receptionist relented a bit. "I will give you the principal's email address," she said. "Have her email him, and in the meantime, fill out the paperwork again and bring it back tomorrow."

When we got home, I went to Erin's house, emailed the principal, and helped her fill out the paperwork once more. Deanna finally got enrolled. It took until the third day of school to finish the registration process, but she went there for her first grade year.

Throughout that year, Erin would send Deanna over to our house if her homework was too difficult for her, her mother or her father to understand. I did not mind helping out. Sometimes the homework was easy, and only required Katie to read some of the words that Deanna had trouble with. Other times, I had to sit down and work with Deanna myself.

One evening, near Thanksgiving, Deanna's homework consisted of a worksheet that had a picture of a turkey on it. The assignment was to draw a disguise on the turkey and write a story about how the disguise helped the turkey avoid being eaten for Thanksgiving. This cute little assignment caused a giant amount of stress to Erin. She came to my door.

"Rahhh Beeen, I don't know what this means. Can Kaley help?"

I looked at the paper.

"Have you guys ever been in the states for Thanksgiving?" I asked. "Do you understand what this holiday is about?"

"No," she replied

"I can help Deanna; not a problem," I said, but it kind of was a problem. My parents and aunt were flying into Tampa that night. They were staying in Florida for two weeks and spending the Thanksgiving holiday with us. That week leading up to their arrival, I had been cleaning the house like a madwoman. When Erin came by, I was trying to make the final preparations for my family's arrival, but when I saw how stressed out she was over Deanna's assignment, I forgot about that for a moment because I understood how confusing this must have been. If you don't have a grasp on a holiday that is turkey-centric, how can you possibly understand putting a disguise on a cartoon turkey and making up a story about it?

Katie and Joel did their best to explain the assignment to Deanna, but they grew impatient. I looked at the paper. Deanna had drawn jewelry and a tiara on the turkey with crayon.

"Is this the turkey's disguise?" I asked.

"Yes, she is a princess," Deanna said proudly.

"That is a great disguise," I said. "Now let's work on a story for this turkey. Do you know about eating turkey on Thanksgiving?"

"No," she replied.

"Okay," I answered. "Well, next week there is a holiday called Thanksgiving. To celebrate it, we all eat turkey. This turkey on your paper doesn't want to get eaten, right?"

"Right," said Deanna, smiling and looking at me with her giant brown eyes and her frizzy hair standing on end. My heart melted.

"Now, how will a turkey dressing up like a princess save her from getting eaten? Do people want to eat a princess?" I asked, feeding her the idea for a story.

"No, they want dance with a princess," she replied.

"Very good! I like that." I said. Deanna's face brightened.

"That's a great idea for a story," I told her. "The turkey doesn't want to get eaten, so she dresses like a princess, so everyone will want to dance with her, not eat her. Now how should we start this story? What would be a really good first sentence?"

Deanna beamed and replied, "There once was a princess."

"Well," I said, choosing my words carefully. "Remember that this turkey only dresses up to be a princess, so she doesn't get eaten. She doesn't start out being a princess; she starts out being a turkey. Let's think of a better first sentence for this story, okay?"

"Okay," Deanna said, still smiling.

"What would be a good way to start this story?" I coaxed.

"There once was a princess..." Deanna said again.

At that point, I basically gave her the first sentence. I did not want to write it for her, but I was not sure how long this was going to take. My parents were going to be landing soon, and I still needed to make up everyone's beds with clean sheets.

Around that same holiday break, Katie asked me to walk her over to Deanna's house. Katie was bored and wanted someone to play with. When I knocked on the door, Erin answered, weeping and holding mail in her hand. Her husband, Clive, was inside the house, also crying.

"Rahh Beeen!" Erin exclaimed, wiping away her tears. "I am sorry we are crying, but we just received such good news today." She held up the papers she had been reading. "We got residency in the United States. We can now leave the country and come back."

"Oh," I said, trying to grasp the situation. "You guys became citizens today?"

"No, our application for residency was accepted. Clive's parents are getting ill, he wants to go to Italy but he can't come back to the United States until we get this paper. We have waited so long for this." Erin choked up again. "This is such a relief for us."

Clive began cheering and speaking in what sounded like happy Italian words, and Erin cried some more.

Their excitement and emotion were contagious. I felt on the verge of tears from just being witness to that scene, but as a comic, expressing such healthy empathy is not possible for me. I sucked it in, congratulated them, and went back home.

Clive, Erin, and Deanna restored my faith in this country—and in humanity, to some extent. As an American, I feel inundated with radio shows, newspapers, websites, magazines, and even television networks constantly telling us what is wrong with the country today and how our nation isn't what it is used to be. None of that was an issue to my neighbors. They did not complain that people sometimes treated them differently because their English was not perfect. They never pointed out the faults of living in the United States. They did not bitch about the recession, or the Tea Party, or Obama, or healthcare, or the debt ceiling, or any of the other issues for which Americans are divided. They openly wept to be living in the land of the free and the home next to me.

Chapter Sixteen
The Poop at Publix

As a kid, I remember hearing that California was full of crazy people. "They are all fruits and nuts," was a phrase frequently used to describe the residents of the Golden State. Somehow, through the years, Florida has taken that title. I do not know if people have gotten crazier, or if the relentless heat and humidity takes its toll on the collective sanity of its citizens. But anytime a weird news article makes the national headlines, Florida is always the state where the weird unfolded. In which state did a lady call the cops when McDonalds ran out of McNuggets and a topless lady ransacked a location of the same chain, taking a short break to eat ice cream directly out of the soft serve machine? In which state did a guy who loves Fox News so much stab his girlfriend for being too liberal? In which state did a lady get arrested for riding a manatee, and of course, where did a classic rogue monkey keep mysteriously showing up in residential neighborhoods? In the epitome of wackiness—the Sunshine State, of course. By the way, the monkey developed such a following that people were actually rooting for the primate. Some wanted him to stay a fugitive-at-large forever, and someone even made a Facebook page for him. To this day, he has 85,178 followers. That is Florida for you—a little bit of redneck, a little bit of East Coast, a little bit of retired folks, a little bit of Spanish flair, a tiny bit of wild animals, and a whole lot of crazy!

Grocery shopping in my Florida neighborhood is always an experience and can border on the crazy. The best store in the area is the Publix. It is pricier than the others, but it has a good selection and seemingly real food. We have plenty of "questionable" stores nearby. There is an Aldi across the street and a Bravo a few blocks away. Aldi is a German supermarket chain that keeps overhead low by selling only generic foods, charging shoppers a refundable quarter as an incentive to return their shopping carts, and having the customers bag their own groceries (they charge for the bags, too, unless you bring your own canvas tote). No one ever openly admits to shopping there. If you run into a neighbor in an aisle, you just exchange silent glances of mutual shame.

The Bravo used to be a U-Save Supermarket. I don't trust a business that doesn't fully spell the word "You." I don't know if it originally seemed clever to use this alternative spelling, or if excluding the extra two letters, "YO," on the sign saved money. Maybe with the success of Toys R Us, the founders of this store thought they would try it too. It really didn't work, since Bravo ended up ultimately taking over the store. Bravo also doesn't live up to its name either. It is fairly run-down and does not garner any kind of applause for shopping there.

So, back to Publix. One particular Sunday morning a few years ago, I was craving a bagel and some coffee. I waited until 8 AM and then took my daughter to Publix to buy the fixings for a "continental" breakfast (we are fancy like that). We were rounding the aisle to the refrigerated section to get the cream cheese when we saw it—a giant blob of poop on the floor. "Eeww," my little girl called out. "Mommy, what is that?"

I am not a feces expert by any means, but having spent a good deal of my childhood on a farm, I can say with certainty that I can differentiate human poop from animal poop. This was not animal manure. Besides, the only animal allowed in a grocery store on a Sunday morning would have to have been some type of service dog. Dog droppings are identifiable as small oval-type pellets. This was a big pile of crap. It had to have been "person" excrement—which led to the inevitable questions: Who, why, and most importantly how would someone have taken a massive Number Two on Publix's floor?

Again, I don't have a Dr. Oz Ph.D on BMs, but as a former (and sometimes current) drinker, I would say this could easily have been a case of Sunday morning "beer shits." It was runny and dark, like the after effects of a PBR night. (I know that brand of beer is big with the hipsters these days, but there is nothing cool about having your bowels wrung out from the previous night's entertainment.) As for the "how," I wondered: Did someone just come in with the intention of using the restrooms? Maybe they had tried to hold it in and realized they just could not make it, then "dropped trou" and crapped right on the floor. Maybe they were so embarrassed that they ran out of the store, never to return or to drink cheap beer again.

Or maybe it was a disgruntled Publix worker—a bag boy of German descent who desperately wanted the store to utilize the Aldi's model of efficiency, but alas, had to bag the groceries and collect the carts, day in and day out, and finally one morning decided out of frustration to make a big "scheisse" at the front of Aisle #7. Or perhaps it was a cashier who had been trying to get promoted to working in the deli department, but had constantly been passed over due to her lack of meat-cutting experience. "How about you slice this loaf, bitches," she thought while defiling the freshly mopped tile floor. Both employees would have known the routine and would have been aware that the morning crew would be too busy doing their opening duties to notice. Both would have known when no one would be around that area and could simply have found their opportunity, pulled down their pants underneath their green smock, assumed the squatting position and let loose.

I also wondered, was there a look-out person? If so, how would you ask someone to be your pooping wingman? How would that conversation go? Would it be something like, "Hey, man, I am not happy with my current working conditions, so I am going take a dump on the floor this morning. Could you come with me and make sure no one is around? It won't take long. I drank PBR last night."

Maybe it was one of the nearby homeless people. I would think that for homeless men, peeing would not be that hard—they could just find a tree or look for a dumpster and "go" behind it, but homeless women and men who have to make a deuce do require restroom facilities. I believe homeless people would not be so disrespectful as to shit on a floor; for them, learning which establishments have the best bathrooms and will give them the least amount of hassle about using the "commode" is a big part of their daily lives.

There is a homeless guy who lives within a 10-mile radius of the Publix. I see him everywhere. He used to always sit near a bus stop with a detailed sign that explained how he had won the Pennsylvania Lottery, but they never paid him his winnings. I am not sure how he ended up in Tampa, Florida. He is very red-faced, with long white hair and a long white beard. My kids deemed him "Grumpy Old Troll," after the character on the "Dora The Explorer" television show who guards a bridge unless you solve a riddle. I don't think our Grumpy Old Troll quizzes people who walk down the sidewalk, unless, of course, it's about the whereabouts of his Pennsylvania lottery winnings.

But I can almost guarantee that it wasn't Grumpy Old Troll who pooped on the floor that morning. He had dignity. He obviously has a hard life, but he is a man of conviction. He sincerely believes he has been jilted by the state of Pennsylvania and has stuck to his guns. Plus, I think if he were to shit anywhere, it would be on something related to that state—maybe a Pirates baseball hat, or a Bruins shirt, or a picture of the Liberty Bell.

I think the pooping culprit was a younger person, either a teenager or college-aged person. Pooping is such a source of entertainment, especially to younger men. I must admit that I do not know why it is considered such a comedy staple. Not every bodily function is met with that much amusement. Maybe farting is regarded as a laugh-inducer, but really, it is just Poop's little brother. Belching takes a weak third place. Belching is like the Ringo Starr of funny bodily functions. It is okay, but the other two kill every time. There was a whole segment in one of the "Jackass" movies where the band of idiots featured in the film goes to a hardware store and shits in the display toilet. (Those movies grossed millions, while stand up comics work continually to write and perform witty and fresh material. Who knew that all it took to get big laughs was to empty your bowels in an inappropriate setting?)

Culprits and the comedy of pooping aside, we continued our shopping that morning, but I kept checking back in at the "scene of the crime." The management was alerted, not by me. I was an observer. I did not want to become involved. My fascination was to see how it all played out, like a camera man filming the wildlife of Africa. Yeah, I felt bad seeing the lame zebra devoured by the lions, but it wasn't my place to interfere, just to monitor and someday report.

Once the store authorities became involved, it got serious. There were at least four employees standing around the mound of dookie. Most were wearing Oxford-type long-sleeved shirts and name badges, which in the world of grocery stores indicates "Management Level." At one point, they got fluorescent orange cones and blocked off the offending "matter." I wondered if they contacted the police or checked the surveillance tapes. I wondered whether, if they were able to figure out who had done it, charges would be pressed. I imagined that at best, the charges would just be for some sort of minor misdemeanor—unless a person was a serial public (or Publix, as it were) pooper, in which case it would require some sort of psychiatric evaluation. Is one so suppressed with rage that the only way they can show their discontent with the world is to shit in as many common areas as they can find?

I think the absolute worst part of the story is the person who had to eventually clean the poop up. You know it was the lowest employee on the totem pole—the one with the lowest level of seniority. It wasn't any of the managers cleaning it up; they would have been above doing the vile work. Besides, what better time to demonstrate authority than to be in a crowd, shouting, "This is outrageous. We will get to the bottom of this. Get the new guy. What's his name, Barry? Get him. Have Barry clean this up. " In the meantime, Barry is fuming. "They want me to pick up what???" he yells. "Fuck that. I don't get paid enough to pick up a watery pile of shit at 8 AM. I do not need this job that damn bad."

Since my daughter was very young at the time, common sense would have dictated that I not bother her with my many questions about the incident. Sadly, common sense took a second to my morbid fascination. "How do you think it got there?" I asked my then-six-year-old.

"Gross, Mommy, stop talking about it," she said. "It makes me sick to think about."

"Yeah, but it was just right there, right in the open," I continued.

"Stop, Mommy!"

"Sorry, Honey. I am just really curious about it. You think someone would have seen something?"

"STOP!"

To this day, I still do not know how it happened. It is not something you can ask about. You cannot nonchalantly bring it up to the cashier on your next visit, asking, "Hey, so how did that mystery pile of crap play out?" Maybe the rest of the employees did not even know about it. Maybe the crew working that morning was told to by management to downplay the whole thing. You know that behind closed doors, though, everyone was talking about it. Someone probably even took a picture of it that morning and texted it to a coworker: "Sheila, this is what happens when I agree to trade shifts with you. I hope brunch with your Nana was worth me having to forego my dignity and clean this mess up. I am so over this place-Barry."

So I do not ask. I do not want to draw suspicion to myself and my borderline obsessive interest in a disgusting moment in time. I just go about my day, with so many unanswered questions and the knowledge that there are public poopers walking amongst us.

About the Author:

Robin Savage is a Mother of two school-aged children by day and a Stand-Up comedian by night. She has been known to mix the two up and offer her kids a two-item minimum while helping a heckler with his homework. Robin has played comedy clubs and festivals across the country. She won a Best Actress award for a comedy short that she co-wrote in the 2014 St. Pete Comedy Film Festival. When Robin isn't performing comedy, she can be seen, late at night, Googling her own name.